CROCHETiNG CLOTHES KiDS LOVE

Creative Publishing international

First published in the United States of America by
Creative Publishing international, Inc., a member of
Quayside Publishing Group
400 First Avenue North
Suite 400
Minneapolis, MN 55401
1-800-328-3895
www.creativepub.com
Visit www.Craftside.Typepad.com for a behind-the-scenes peek at our crafty world!

ISBN: 978-1-58923-781-0

10 9 8 7 6 5 4 3 2 1

Library of Congress Cataloging-in-Publication Data available

Technical Editor: Karen Manthey
Copy Editor: Kari Cornell
Proofreader: Julie Grady
Book Design: Kathie Alexander
Cover Design: CPI
Page Layout: Kathie Alexander
Illustrations: Karen Manthey
Photographs: Nancy J. S. Langdon
Rau + Barber (pg. 64, 138)

Printed in China

CROCHETiNG CLOTHES KiDS LOVE

INCLUDES 28 FUN-TO-WEAR PROJECTS

Creative Publishing
international

contents

Introduction

Crochet and children's wear is a great match, and writing this book together was an amazing experience. We were each able to collaborate on designs we love, and the end result was this special book. Our sincere hope is that we've created a collection of projects that crocheters and the children for whom they crochet will enjoy for years to come. The concept of the book is unique because it focuses on children between 6 and 12 years of age. This age group is often overlooked, as the majority of children's patterns are designed for babies and toddlers. This is surprising, because we found the possibilities for children's wear design to be exciting and vast.

Crocheting for children is appealing since the projects are of a small scale, so they don't take a lot of time or yarn to complete. Children of this age are old enough to appreciate the effort and love that goes into making something by hand especially for them, and will wear the items with pride.

If you would like to learn new techniques or stitch patterns, making clothes and accessories for children is a wonderful way to gain experience. The projects in our book feature details and embellishments made from simple techniques that can be used in myriad ways. Feel free to use the patterns as a jumping off point, and customize the pieces to match the personality of the child. Make your project truly unique by choosing a new color, adjusting the length, and adding more or using fewer details or embellishments. Techniques in this book include: appliqué, colorwork, surface crochet, Tunisian crochet, and unconventional hook placement.

We hope that this book will be a useful source of inspiration and instruction that you will turn to often to crochet much-loved gifts for the children in your life.

—Shelby Allaho and Ellen Gormley

chapter 1

Crocheting
for Kids

Gauge

It certainly would be easier to ignore gauge and just start stitching, but why take the gamble on your hard-earned project? Gauge is the number of stitches per inch. The gauge number given in a pattern in conjunction with the yarn and hook specified will give you the ingredients you need to make the best possible project. This information is important for three main reasons. You want your project to fit, you want the project to have the right drape, and you don't want to run out of yarn. Reading the gauge information carefully for each project before you begin will help ensure that you are taking a calculated risk that will lead to a WIN.

Getting the correct number of stitches per inch in a project is important for fit because it all adds up! If the pattern specifies that you need 16 stitches per 4 inches, but your swatch or project is measuring 16 stitches in 3½ inches, there is a half-inch difference. That extra half inch may not seem like a big deal, but multiply it by several inches for a sweater or hat and that half-inch shortfall will shrink your project. It may shrink the finished product so much that it is uncomfortable or it can't even be worn! Continuing with the example of a pattern that calls for 16 stitches per 4 inches, what if you were only getting 14 stitches per 4 inches? Is it ok to go ahead and start your project now? Only if you want your project to be too big! If you are fitting in 14 stitches in 4 inches where 16 stitches are supposed to fit… then your stitches are bigger than they are supposed to be. Following the pattern with stitches that are too big, the project will turn out larger than planned.

While the gauge on the yarn band may offer a suggestion of what size hook to use, it is just a suggestion. The designer chooses a hook size based on what kind of "drape" or flexibility of fabric she wants to achieve. For a skirt, it may be an advantage to have a more flexible, drapey flowing fabric, where a bag or tote might be better in a denser, stiffer, less drapey fabric. Choose the hook listed in the pattern first for a project that will more closely resemble the project in the photo.

Who hasn't run out of yarn for a project only to find that the store is sold out or only has the wrong dye lot left in stock? If your stitches are too big or too small, you may end up using more yarn, working through your yarn investment more quickly, leaving you short before the project is complete. Remember to not only buy enough yarn for the complete project, but enough to make a gauge swatch before beginning.

You'll know it's time to start the project when your swatch matches the pattern gauge. Begin by swatching with the yarn and hook specified in the pattern. How does it compare to the gauge listed? If your stitches are too big, try going down a hook size. If your stitches are too small, try going up a hook size. Because all stitchers make stitches slightly differently, some will have stitches that are more tightly made and some more loosely made. To make adjustments to match gauge, the first thing to play with is hook size. It's the easiest way to get closer to gauge. When you have found the right hook to achieve gauge, make a note of it on your pattern and begin!

Sizing

Though many crocheters are nervous to make the leap from accessories to garments, it need not be an intimidating jump. The biggest hurdle with garments is achieving gauge so that the time is not wasted and the wearer gets to enjoy the project.

Once you have done a large gauge swatch in the stitch pattern for the project you want to make, it's time to look at the sizes provided in the pattern. Just as adults come in different shapes and sizes, so do children. Children's sizes are based on their age. At stores, when you buy for babies, toddlers, and children, you typically choose the garment size that matches the child's age. After toddlerhood, children begin to vary more in size. Parents usually know if their child is "big for his age" or "small for his age." This helps them choose clothes when the child is not available to try them on. Garments in knit and crochet are listed by size according to small, medium, and large, with additional information about specific measurements to help define those terms.

For the purposes of this book, finished measurements are provided for each project. The term "finished measurements" means that when the garment is complete, stitched to gauge, and blocked according to the instructions, it should match the finished measurements provided. Keep in mind that if the finished measurements say that the small measures 28" (71 cm) in the chest, then it probably will *not* fit comfortably on a child with a 28" (71 cm) chest. For the projects in this book, we've added extra inches to the finished measurements, allowing the wearer to move freely and feel comfortable. The best way to choose a size for a child is to measure him or her with a tape measure. Write that number down and consider the type of garment. Is it a layering vest where the child will wear another shirt or garment underneath it? Or is it a one-layer item that will be worn next to the skin? Generally, for a child's garment, choose a finished size that is 2" to 3" (5 to 7.5 cm) larger than the child's actual size. For heavier items such as sweaters and coats that are meant to be worn over other garments, 3" to 4" (7.5 to 10 cm) might be more appropriate.

If you are unable to take measurements of the recipient, then either ask the parent to measure or ask for the child's current clothing size. You can decide to go up to the next size if you think the garment will take a while to complete, or, if you are a speedy stitcher, choose to make the child's current size.

If the child is a size 6 in store clothes, how does that size convert to a crochet pattern? If the pattern gives both pieces of information: size 6 is finished 26" (66 mm) for example, and you know your recipient is of pretty average size, then you are good to go. If a pattern only states size 6 but offers specific measurements, you can visit www.yarnstandards.com and look at the sizing charts for different ages. The table will tell you, for example, that a child of 6 (on average) has a chest size of 25" (63.5 cm).

With a great swatch and a little investigating, you'll be able to choose the right size and stitch so the child will love to wear it.

Choosing Yarn for Children's Garments and Accessories

Yarn choice is one of the most important elements of a project's success. It directly affects how much you enjoy making an item, how much it will appeal to the child who will be wearing it, how comfortable it will be to wear, how easy it is to care for, and how long it will look its best.

The yarns for the projects in this book were chosen based on the following considerations:

- The type of garment or accessory, and for what season it was intended. Cotton yarns provide a lovely sheen and stitch definition to accessories like jewelry and hairbands, and are perfect for summer garments. Wool is durable and it will keep children warm in the winter. Good quality acrylic yarn is a popular, year-round choice for children's items, because it is easy to care for.
- Ease of care. All of the garments and the majority of the accessories in this book are made from machine washable yarns. The projects you make should be worn often and enjoyed by the child you make them for. You want the items to be worn, not just saved for special occasions!
- Texture. Softness is very important when making things for children. No child wants to wear something they find itchy. Cotton, washable wool, and acrylic yarns are all comfortable to wear.
- Yarn weight. The yarns we used range from sport to worsted weight. Yarns that aren't too bulky work well with the scale of children's items.
- Color. Color is an important factor in the success and appeal of children's wear. We chose yarns that were available in a wide range of beautiful colors.

- Price. We selected yarns in a variety of price ranges, from yarns that can be purchased at large chain stores, to those only available through specialty yarn shops websites.

It is possible to substitute yarns that you may already have, or that you find more readily available, but you must make sure that the yarn weight is the same as the one used in the book. In addition, the stitches per inch should match the yarn used in the book, exactly. This information can be found on the yarn label. It is a good idea to compare yarn label information for the yarn used in the book to the yarn you would like to use. If you want your projects to look very similar to the projects in the book, you must choose yarn with the same fiber content and qualities. Things to look for are: texture, amount of sheen, how many plies (strands) are combined to make the yarn, and how they are plied (twisted together). The amount of plies a yarn has and how tightly they are plied determines the amount of stitch definition you will get. A tightly plied multi-ply yarn, for example, will yield more stitch definition than a loosely plied yarn with fewer plies. Note that two yarns can have the same number of plies, but be different yarn weights.

One final note: Get the child involved in the process, if you can. Let him or her choose the yarn colors for the project. If a bit of their personality goes into color choice, the resulting piece will be one that they will love and wear often.

Blocking

The best way to achieve a professional finish on a crochet project is to block it. Blocking is a water or steam process that makes the stitches even and sets the fabric to the finished measurements. Blocking is generally done when a project is complete or before garment pieces are assembled, and any time the finished project is cleaned after use. If you have never blocked your crocheted items before, you may not see the need to block. It is certain though, that if you invest the time in blocking, it will pay off. You will notice many benefits to blocking your crocheted items. Blocking relaxes the fibers and improves the drape of the fabric. It can shrink or stretch the fabric depending on how you pin it to the blocking board. You will be able to make small adjustments to the length and width of a piece and even out the edges for a better shape. This is very helpful, especially if your gauge has changed slightly when crocheting the different components of a project. Blocking works wonders with lace and other motifs, opening up the designs to show their true beauty.

While blocking is a magical process and improves most every crocheted fabric, take care not to over block and flatten textural design features. Stretching pieces too far beyond their limit can reduce the visual impact of features such as cables and surface crochet.

Before blocking, check the fiber content on the label of the yarn you used to determine whether to wet or steam block. In general, cotton yarns can be wet blocked or blocked with warm/hot steam. Wool yarns can be wet blocked by spraying with water or steam blocked with warm steam. It is best for synthetic yarns to only be wet blocked by spraying with water, since heat might damage the crocheted fabric. When in doubt as to the best way to block a project, try out different methods with the gauge swatch.

You will need the following supplies to block a finished garment.
- A blocking surface. For small projects, a padded ironing board will be sufficient, but for larger projects, you will need a blocking board or blocking mats.
- Rust-proof pins, T-pins, or pins with glass heads, if steam blocking
- Tape measure or ruler
- Spray bottle for wet blocking or steam iron for steam blocking
- Press cloth for steam blocking, to avoid damaging the texture or sheen of the yarn

To Wet Block

1. On the blocking surface, pin the piece(s) out into the desired shape and size to match the schematic or finished measurements listed on the pattern.
2. Next, spray with cool water to wet the pieces thoroughly. Alternatively, you can soak the piece(s) in cool water, then squeeze out the excess without twisting or wringing, and pin them out as mentioned previously.
3. Allow all pieces to dry before removing pins.

To Steam Block

1. Set your iron to the steam setting, or heat up your hand-held steamer. Adjust the heat setting according to the fiber content of the yarn used.
2. Pin the piece(s) out according to the wet block method, and cover with a press cloth.
3. With the hand-held steamer, go over all areas of the piece(s) without touching the surface. Remove the press cloth.
4. Allow all pieces to dry before removing pins.

Tips and Tricks

As we were writing this book, we jotted down a few tips and tricks that may be helpful as you crochet our patterns.

- Always make a gauge swatch before beginning a project. Before measuring the swatch, block it as you would the finished item.

- If you are someone who crochets tightly, consider using a hook that is a size or two larger for the beginning chain. To choose a hook size, look at the size of the loops in the last row of your gauge swatch and use the hook that will help you yield that size. By doing this, the first row will be easier to work, and your first and last row will be the same length.

- When making an adjustable ring (page 15), don't make it much larger than the size you need to fit in all of your stitches. It can be difficult to tighten it neatly and easily if the loops are too big.

- When a pattern calls for a color change, change colors in the last step of the last stitch in the previous color (use the new color for the final yarn over, and pull it through the work).

- When it is time to block your project, refer to the finished measurements on the schematic, and pin the pieces to the correct size.

- Feel free to experiment with color. Customize the projects to make the project one of a kind.

- When weaving in ends, weave the end for an inch or two in one direction, then weave another inch or two in the opposite direction. Check the front of the project to make sure the end doesn't show through.

- Take a photo of yourself with the recipient wearing your handmade project.

- Children between ages 6 and 12 are at a perfect age to learn crochet! Get the child involved in the process of choosing the yarn, colors, and embellishments. Encourage the child's natural curiosity.

- Keep leftover yarn bands along with a photo of the finished project in a binder in the laundry room. This will give you easy access to washing instructions when and where you need them, and you'll know which instructions go with which project.

- Make sibling projects for siblings! Change up details, colors, and embellishments to make them unique but still harmonious.

- Fully read a pattern through before beginning. Practice any special stitches or techniques on your swatch.

- After completing a project, takes some notes! What did you learn? What would you do differently? Make note of the yarn you chose and your experience with it.

Special Techniques

Invisible Fasten Off

Cut the yarn, leaving a 3" (7.5 cm) tail. Insert the hook into the blo of the first st in rnd, yo, and pull the yarn all the way through the loop on the hook, as if to fasten off in the usual way. Insert the hook in both lps of next st, yo with tail end and pull through st. Finally, insert the hook in the flo of last st in rnd, yo, pull yarn down through.

Magic Ring

Also called adjustable ring or sliding ring, this method of beginning to crochet in the round allows you to pull the ring tightly closed.

Wrap the yarn clockwise around your index finger twice, leaving a 6" (15.2 cm) tail. Holding the tail between your thumb and another finger, slide the hook under the wraps and catch the working yarn. Pull the working yarn through the ring, yarn over, and through both loops on hook. Work specified stitches into the two loops of the ring, keeping the tail free. Before joining in the round, pull on the loop that tightens the ring (pulling on the other loop shortens the tail). The other loop will slacken. Then pull the tail to tighten the remaining loop.

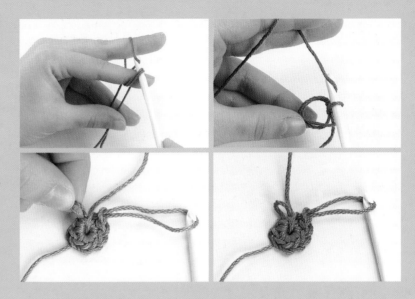

Foundation Single Crochet (fsc)

Start with a slip knot on hook, ch 2, insert hook in 2nd ch from hook, draw up a lp, yo, draw through 1 lp (ch made), yo, and draw through 2 lps—1 single crochet with its own chain at bottom. Work next stitch under lps of that chain. Insert hook under 2 lps at bottom of the previous stitch, draw up a lp, yo and draw through 1 lp, yo and draw through 2 lps. Repeat for length of foundation.

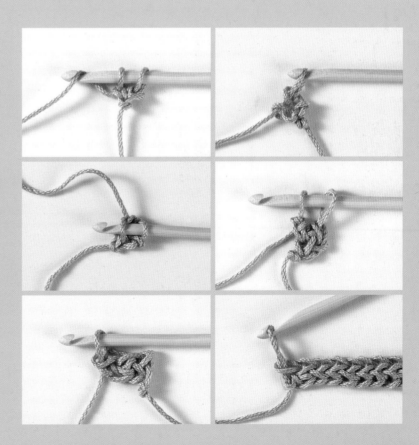

Abbreviations

beg	beginning		sk	skip
bet	between		Sl st	slip stitch
blo	back loop only		sp(s)	space(s)
BPdc	back post double crochet		ssc	short single crochet
bo	bind off		st(s)	stitch(es)
ch	chain		tr	triple crochet
ch-:	refers to chain or space previously made, e.g., ch-1 space		tss	Tunisian simple stitch
			tss2tog	Tunisian simple stitch decrease (two together)
CL	cluster		tws	twisted simple stitch
cm	centimeter		WS	wrong side of work
dc	double crochet		yo	yarn over (wrap the yarn around the hook)
dc2tog	double crochet decrease		[ ]	Work instructions within brackets as many times as directed
dec	decrease			
ehdc	extended half double crochet		( )	Work instructions within parentheses as many times as directed
fdc	foundation double crochet			
flo	front loop only		*	Repeat instructions following the single asterisk as directed
foll	follow/follows/following			
FP	front post		* *	Repeat instructions between asterisks as many times as directed or repeat from a given set of instructions
FPdc	front post double crochet			
FPhdc	front post half double crochet			
FPtr	front post treble crochet			
fsc	foundation single crochet			
g	gram(s)			
hdc	half double crochet			
hdc2tog	half double crochet 2 together			
inc	increase			
lp(s)	loop(s)			
long sc	long single crochet			
m	meter(s)			
mm	millimeter(s)			
oz	ounce(s)			
patt	pattern			
pm	place marker			
rem	remaining			
rep	repeat			
rev sc	reverse single crochet			
rnd(s)	round(s)			
RS	right side of work			
sc	single crochet			
sc2tog	single crochet 2 stitches together			
sdc	short double crochet			
shdc	short half double crochet			

Term Conversions

Crochet techniques are the same universally, and everyone uses the same terms. However, US patterns and UK patterns are different because the terms denote different stitches. Here is a conversion chart to explain the differences.

US	UK
single crochet (sc)	double crochet (dc)
half double crochet (hdc)	half treble (htr)
double crochet (dc)	treble (tr)
triple crochet (tr)	double treble (dtr)

chapter 2

About Town

Violet's Tank

A gorgeous edging and corsage make this every day tank a special occasion. Adjust this tank into a dress by working several more inches of the beginning two rows before decreasing. Wear over a long t-shirt or turtleneck for a winter wear option.

Skill Level
Easy

Finished Size
Directions are given for girl's size 4. Changes for 6, 8, 10, and 12 are in parentheses.

Finished Chest: 25 (27, 28, 30, 32)" (63.5 [68.5, 71, 76, 81.5] cm)

Finished Length: 12¾ (13¾, 16, 17¾, 18 ¾)" (32 [35, 40.5, 45, 47.5] cm)

Gauge
18 sts and 16 rows = 4" (10 cm). Take time to check gauge.

Yarn

Classic Elite Provence light weight cotton yarn, 205 yd (187 m), 3.5 oz (100 g): 2 (2, 3, 3, 3) hanks of #2663 Sunny Side Up (A), 1 hank of #2617 Heliotrope (B)

Tools
G/6 (4 mm) crochet hook
yarn needle

Special Stitches Used

- *single crochet 2 together (sc2tog)*
  [Insert hook in next st, yo, draw yarn through st] twice, yo, draw yarn through 3 loops on hook.

Notes: Sc through front loop only of every stitch except the first and last st of every row. Sc through both loops of first and last st of every row.

BACK

With A, ch 69 (73, 77, 81, 85).

Row 1 (RS): Working in back bars of ch sts, sc in 2nd ch from hook and in each ch across, turn—68 (72, 76, 80, 84) sc.

Row 2: Ch 1, sc in both lps of first st, sc in blo of each st across to last st, sc in both lps of last st, turn.

Row 3 (dec row): Ch 1, sc in both lps of first st, sc-2tog in blo of next 2 sts, sc in blo of each st across to last 3 sts, sc2tog in blo of next 2 sts, sc in both lps of last st, turn—66 (70, 74, 78, 82) sts.

Rows 4–23: Dec 1 st at each of every 4th row (5 times)—56 (60, 64, 68, 72) sts.

Rows 24–29 (31, 43, 41, 47): Work even on 56 (60, 64, 68, 72) sc.

Armhole Shaping

Row 1: Ch 1, sl st in first 8 (8, 9, 9, 9) sts, ch 1, sc in flo of next st and each st across to last 8 (8, 9, 9, 9) sts, leaving them unworked—38 (42, 44, 48, 52) sts.

Rows 2–15 (17, 18, 19, 20): Work even on 38 (42, 44, 48, 52) sc.

Shape Neck and First Shoulder

Row 1: Ch 1, sc in each of first 14 sts, sl st in both lps of next st, turn, leaving rem sts unworked—14 sc.

Row 2: Ch 1, sk first sl st, sk first sc, sc in each st across, turn—13 sc.

Row 3: Ch 1, sc in each of first 12 sts, sl st in next st, turn—12 sc.

Row 4: Ch 1, sk first sl st, sk next sc, sc in each st across, turn—11 sc.

Row 5: Ch 1, sc in each of first 9 sts, sl st in next st, turn—10 sc.

Row 6: Ch 1, sk first sl st, sc in each st across, turn—9 sc.

Rows 7–8: Ch 1, turn, sc in each st across. Fasten off, leaving a 6" (15 cm) sewing length.

Shape Neck and Second Shoulder

Row 1: Sk next 8 (12, 14, 18, 22) sts to the left of First Shoulder, join A in next st, sc in next st and in each st across, turn—14 sc.

Row 2: Ch 1, sc in each of first 13 sts, sl st in next st, turn—13 sc.

Row 3: Ch 1, sk first sl st, sk first sc, sc in each st across, turn—12 sc.

Row 4: Ch 1, sc in each of first 11 sts, sl st in next st, turn—11 sc.

Row 5: Ch 1, sk first sl st, sk next sc, sc in each st across, turn—10 sc.

Row 6: Ch 1, sc in each of first 9 sts, sl st in next st, turn—9 sc).

Rows 7–8: Ch 1, turn, sc in each st across. Fasten off, leaving a 6" (15 cm) sewing length.

FRONT

Work same as Back until 13 (15, 16, 17, 18) rows have been worked after armhole shaping—38 (42, 44, 48, 52) sc.

Shape Neck and First Shoulder

Work same as Back through Row 6. Fasten off, leaving a 6"(15 cm) sewing length

Shape Neck and Second Shoulder

Work same as Back through Row 6. Fasten off, leaving a 6" (15 cm) sewing length.

FINISHING

With RS of Front and Back facing, and using yarn tails, whipstitch shoulder seams. Mattress st the side seams. Turn RS out.

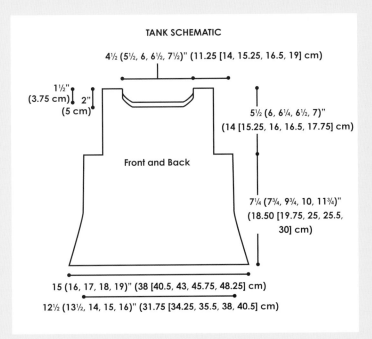

TANK SCHEMATIC

4½ (5½, 6, 6½, 7½)" (11.25 [14, 15.25, 16.5, 19] cm)

1½" (3.75 cm)

2" (5 cm)

5½ (6, 6¼, 6½, 7)" (14 [15.25, 16, 16.5, 17.75] cm)

Front and Back

7¼ (7¾, 9¾, 10, 11¾)" (18.50 [19.75, 25, 25.5, 30] cm)

15 (16, 17, 18, 19)" (38 [40.5, 43, 45.75, 48.25] cm)

12½ (13½, 14, 15, 16)" (31.75 [34.25, 35.5, 38, 40.5] cm)

BOTTOM EDGING

Note: Edgings require a multiple of 5 sts.

Hem

With RS facing, working across opposite side of foundation ch, join A with a sc in first ch to the left of side seam, work 134 (144, 149, 159, 169) more sc evenly spaced around bottom edge, join with a sl st in first sc—135 (145, 150, 160, 170) sc. Fasten off A, join B.

Rnd 2: With B, ch 1, sc in each sc around.

Rnd 3: *(Ch 5, sl st, ch 7, sl st, ch 5, sl st) in same st, sl st in next 5 sts; rep from * around—27 (29, 30, 32, 34) sets of 3 lps. Fasten off.

ARMHOLE EDGING

Rnd 1: With RS facing, join A with a sc in bottom of one underarm, sc in each st and row-end st around, join with a sl st in first sc. Fasten off A, join B.

Rnd 2: With B, (ch 1, sl st) in each st around. Fasten off.

Rep Armhole Edging around second armhole.

NECKLINE EDGING

Rnd 1: With RS facing, join A with a sc in center back neck, sc in each st and row-end st around, join with a sl st in first sc. Fasten off A, join B.

Rnd 2: With B, (ch 1, sl st) in each st around. Fasten off.

Weave in ends.

FLOWER

Flower Center

With B, ch 3, join with sl st to form a ring,

Rnd 1: [Sc, ch 2, sc] 5 times in ring, join with a sl st in first sc—5 ch-2 sps. Fasten off.

Middle Layer

With A, ch 5, join with sl st to form a ring,

Rnd 1: Ch 3 (counts as dc), 14 dc in ring, join with a sl st in top beg ch-3.

Rnd 2: *(Ch 5, sl st, ch 7, sl st, ch 5, sl st) in same st, sl st in next 3 sts; rep from * around—5 sets of 3 lps. Fasten off.

Background Layer

With B, ch 5, join with sl st to form a ring

Rnd 1: Ch 3 (counts as dc), 14 dc in ring, join with sl st in top beg ch-3—15 dc.

Rnd 2: Ch 2 (counts as hdc), hdc in same st, 2 hdc in each dc around, join with a sl st in top beg ch-2—30 hdc.

Rnd 3: (Ch 7, sl st, ch 9, sl st, ch 7, sl st) in same st, sl st in each of next 5 sts—6 sets of 3 lps. Fasten off, leaving a 12" (30.5 cm) sewing length.

Stack the flower pieces placing Center on top of Middle Layer and Middle Layer on top of Background Layer. With yarn needle and tail from background, sew layers together, with same tail, sew flower to tank securely. Fasten off.

Steam block to measurements.

Lacy Sundress

Your favorite girl will love the airy twirly-ness in this show-stopping sundress. The feminine stitch pattern is quick and fun to make. Make it in shades of blue and she'll feel like flying. The sky's the limit. The stretchy bodice is perfect for coverage and comfort. The light skirt is perfect for layering and spinning.

Special Stitches Used

- *3-tr cluster (Cl)*
  *Yo (twice), insert hook in indicated st or sp, yo and draw up a loop, [yo, draw through 2 loops on hook] twice; rep from * twice, yo, draw through all 4 loops on hook.

- *beg tr-cluster (Beg Cl)*
  Ch 3, *yo (twice), insert hook in indicated st or sp, yo and draw up a loop, [yo, draw through 2 loops on hook] twice; rep from * once, yo, draw through all 3 loops on hook.

- *picot*
  Ch 3, hdc in 3rd ch from hook.

- *single crochet 2 together (sc2tog)*
  [Insert hook in next st, yo, draw yarn through st] twice, yo, draw yarn through 3 loops on hook.

Skill Level
Intermediate

Finished Size
Directions are given for girl's size 4. Changes for 6, 8, 10, and 12 are in parentheses.

Finished Chest: 22 (24, 25½, 27, 29)" (56 [61, 65, 68.5, 73.5] cm)

Finished Length: 17½ (18, 21½, 22¼, 26)" (44.5 [45.5, 54.5, 56.6, 66] cm) excluding Ties

Gauge
20 sts and 23 rows in sc in blo patt = 4" (10 cm). Take time to check gauge.

Yarn

Tahki Yarns Cotton Classic Lite, 100% mercerized cotton, 146 yd (133 m)/ 1.75 oz (50 g): 3 (3, 4, 4, 5) hanks of #4870 dark bright blue (A) and 4 (4, 6, 6, 8) hanks of #4812 light blue (B)

Tools
G/6 (4 mm) crochet hook

yarn needle

four ¾" (2 cm) buttons

sewing needle and matching sewing thread

12" (30.5 cm) of ⅞" (22 mm) wide grosgrain ribbon to match yarn A

Notes: The first 5 rows and the last 5 rows of the Bodice are worked in both loops of sts. On the rest of the Bodice, the first and last sts of the rows are worked through both loops, and all other sc are worked in the back loop only.

BODICE

With A, ch 29 (31, 33, 37, 41).

Button Band

Row 1 (RS): Sc in 2nd ch from hook and in each of ch across, turn—28 (30, 32, 36, 40) sc.

Rows 2–5: Ch 1, sc in both loops of each sc across, turn.

Continuing with bodice:

Row 6 (WS): Ch 1, sc in both loops of first sc, sc in blo of each sc across to last st, sc in both loops of last st, turn.

Rows 7–126 (138, 146, 156, 166): Rep Row 6. Do not fasten off.

Buttonhole Band

Rows 1–2: Ch 1, sc in both loops of each sc across, turn.

Row 3 (buttonhole row): Ch 1, sc in next 2 sts, *ch 2, sk next 2 sts, sc in next 5 (6, 6, 8, 9) sts; rep from * twice, ch 2, sk next 2 sts, sc in last 3 (2, 3, 2, 3) sts, turn—4 ch-2 buttonhole spaces made.

Row 4: Ch 1, sc in each st and ch across, turn—28 (30, 32, 36, 40) sc.

Row 5: Ch 1, sc in each st across—28 (30, 32, 36, 40) sc. Fasten off.

SKIRT

Rnd 1 (bottom edging of Bodice): With Buttonhole Band on top, overlap last 5 rows of Bodice (Buttonhole Band) over first 5 rows (Button Band). On bottom edge of Bodice, working through double thickness of Button Bands, join A with a sc in first row-end st of Buttonhole Band, sc in each of next 4 row-end sts of Button Bands, then sc in each row-end st of Bodice around, join with a sl st in first sc—126 (138, 146, 156, 166) sc. Fasten off.

Rnd 2: With right side facing, join B with a sc in first sc, *sc in each of next 41 (19, 20, 30, 54) sts, 2 sc in next st; rep from * 1 (5, 5, 3, 1) times, sc in last 42 (18, 20, 32, 56) sts, join with a sl st in first sc—128 (144, 152, 160, 168) sc.

Rnd 3: Ch 1, sc in first sc, *ch 3, sk next 3 sts, (Cl, ch 7, Cl) in next sc, ch 3, sk next 3 sts**, sc in next st; rep from * around, ending last rep at **, join with a sl st in first sc—16 (18, 19, 20, 21) ch-7 sps.

Rnd 4: Ch 3, sl st in first Cl, ch 3 (advances the yarn to the start of the round), sc in next ch-7 sp, *(Beg Cl in side of sc just made, Cl in next ch-3 sp, ch 1, sk next sc, Cl in next ch-3 sp, Beg Cl in top of Cl just made**, sc in next ch-7 sp; rep from * around, ending last rep at **, join with sl st in first sc.

Rnd 5: Ch 1, sc in first sc, *ch 3, (Cl, ch 7, Cl) in next ch-1 sp, ch 3**, sc in next sc between two horizontal clusters; rep from * around, ending last rep at **, join with a sl st in first sc.

Rnd 6: Sl st in next ch-3 sp, Beg Cl in ch-3 sp, Beg Cl in top of Cl just made, *sc in next ch-7 sp, Beg Cl in side of sc just made, Cl in next ch-3 sp, ch 1**, Cl in next ch-3 sp, beg-cl in Cl just made; rep from * around, ending last rep at **, join with a sl st in top of first Cl.

Rnd 7: Sl st back into ch-1 sp just made, *Beg Cl in ch-1 sp, ch 3, sc in next sc between two horizontal clusters, ch 3, [Cl, ch 7, Cl] in ch-1 sp between Cls, ch 3, Cl in ch-1 sp, ch 7; rep from * around; join with sl st in top first Cl.

Rnd 8: Sl st in next ch-3 sp, Beg Cl in ch-3 sp, *ch 1, Cl in next ch-3 sp, Beg Cl in Cl just made, sc in next ch-7 sp, Beg Cl in side of sc just made**, Cl in next ch-3 sp, ch 1, Cl in next ch-3 sp; rep from * around, ending last rep at **, join with a sl st in first Beg Cl.

Rnd 9: Sl st in next ch-1 sp, (Beg Cl, ch 7, Cl) in ch-1 sp, *ch 3, sc in next sc between horizontal clusters, ch 3**, (Cl, ch 7, Cl) in next ch-1 sp; rep from * around, ending last rep at **; join with a sl st in top first Cl.

Rnd 10: Ch 3 (advances the yarn to the start of the round), sc in next ch-7 sp, *(Beg Cl in side of sc just made, Cl in next ch-3 sp, ch 1, sk next sc, Cl in next ch-3 sp, Beg Cl in top of Cl just made**, sc in next ch-7 sp; rep from * around, ending last rep at **, join with sl st in first sc.

Rnds 11–22 (22, 28, 28, 34): Rep Rnds 5–10 (2 [2, 3, 3, 4]) times.

(continued)

EDGING

Rnd 1: With right side facing, join A with a sl st in first sc of last rnd, ch 1, sc in first sc, *ch 3, (CL, ch 5, Cl) in next ch-1 sp, ch 3**, sc in next sc between two horizontal clusters; rep from * around, ending last rep at **, join with a sl st in first sc.

Rnd 2: Ch 1, sc in first sc, *3 sc in next ch-3 sp, sc in next Cl, (3 sc, picot, 3 sc) in next ch-5 sp, sc in next Cl, 3 sc in next ch-3 sp**, sc in sc; rep from * around, ending last repeat at **, join with a sl st in first sc. Fasten off.

With sewing needle and thread, sew buttons onto one side of grosgrain ribbon, corresponding to buttonhole spacing. Sew the ribbon with the buttons onto the Button Band opposite the buttonholes. Fold under the raw cut edges of the ribbon and tack them into place.

TOP BODICE EDGING

Row 1: With right side facing, join A with a sc in first st of Buttonhole Band, sc in each of next 4 row-end sts of Buttonhole Band, work 59 (67, 75, 75, 83) sc evenly spaced across Bodice to Button Band, working approximately 1 sc in every 2 row-end sts, sc in each of last 5 row-end sts, turn—69 (77, 85, 85, 93) sc. Fasten off.

Arrange the dress on your lap or on a table with the back facing up, the Skirt nearest you, and the Bodice away.

Row 2: With right side facing, join B with a sc in flo of the first st of Row 1, working in flo, *ch 3, sk next 3 sts, (Cl, ch 5, Cl) in next sc**, ch 3, sk next 3 sts, sc in next sc; rep from * around, ending last rep at ** in last st, do not work last sc, turn—9 (10, 11, 11, 12) ch-5 sps.

Row 3: Ch 1, sc in first Cl, *(3 sc, picot, 3 sc) in next ch-5 sp, sc in next Cl, 3 sc in next ch-3 sp, sc in next sc**, 3 sc in next ch-3 sp, sc in next Cl; rep from * around, ending last repeat at **. Fasten off B.

TIES (MAKE 4)

With A, ch 8.

Row 1: Sc in 2nd ch from hook and in each ch across, turn—7 sc.

Rows 2–4: Ch 1, sc in each sc across, turn.

Row 3: Ch 1, sc2tog over first 2 sts, sc in each st to last 2 sts, sc2tog over last 2 sts, turn—5 sc.

Rows 5–8: Ch 1, sc in each st across, turn.

Row 9: Rep Row 3—3 sc.

Rows 10–45: Ch 1, sc in each st across, turn—3 sc.

Tie Edging

Rnd 1: Working across long edge of Tie, sc in each row-end st across to next corner, working across opposite side of foundation ch, sc in each of next 7 ch, working across other long edge of Tie, sc in each row-end st across to next corner, working across top of Row 45, ch 4, sk next sc, (Cl, ch 3, Cl, ch 3, Cl) in next sc, ch 4, sk next sc, join with a sl st in first sc. Fasten off A.

Standard measurements for child's shoulder width are: 9¾ (10¼, 10¾, 11¼, 12)" (25 [26, 27.5, 28.5, 30.5] cm). Place the ties INSIDE those measurements for your size. Lay the dress flat, pin Ties in place and make sure they are evenly paired on the front and back. Fold the dress vertically to find the middle front and make sure the Ties are the same distance to the right and left from the midpoint.

With yarn and yarn needle, sew Ties in place.

Weave in ends.

DRESS SCHEMATIC

6¾ (7¼, 7¾, 8¼, 9)" (17.25 [18.5, 19.75, 20.75, 23] cm)

9¾ (10¼, 10¾, 11¼, 12)" (25 [26, 27.5, 28.75, 30.5] cm)

11" (28 cm)

5½ (6, 6½, 7¼, 8)" (14 [15.25, 16.5, 18.50, 20] cm)

12 (12, 15, 15, 18)" (30.5 [30.5, 38, 38, 45.75] cm)

22 (24, 25½, 27, 29)" (56 [61, 64.74, 68.25, 73.5] cm)

Pretty Popcorn Vest

This fitted lacy vest is a lovely topper for a pretty summer dress. A solid color version is a great basic piece for a girl's wardrobe. You can also make the lace edging in a complementary variegated yarn for a different and fun look.

Special Stitches Used

- **single crochet 2 together (sc2tog)**
  Insert hook in next st, yo, draw yarn through st] twice, yo, draw yarn through 3 loops on hook.

- **3 double crochet cluster (Cl)**
  Yo, insert hook in next sp, yo and draw up a loop, yo, draw through 2 loops on hook] 3 times in same sp, yo, draw yarn through 4 loops on hook.

- **Invisible Fasten Off (page 14)**
  Cut yarn leaving a 3" (7.5 cm) tail. Insert the hook into the blo of the first st in rnd, yo with tail end, and pull the yarn all the way through the loop on the hook, as if to fasten off in the usual way. Insert the hook in both lps of next st, yo with tail end and pull through st. Finally, insert the hook in the flo of last st in rnd, yo, pull yarn down through.

Skill Level
Intermediate

Finished Size
Directions are given for girl's size 6. Changes for 8 and 10 are in parentheses.

Finished Chest: 24 (26, 28)" (61 [66, 71] cm)

Finished Length: 9 (9¾, 10½)" (23 [25, 26.5] cm)

Gauge
21½ sts and 20 rows in sc in flo patt = 4" (10 cm)

Yarn

Berroco Vintage DK, 50% acrylic, 40% wool, 10% nylon, 288 yd (263 m)/3.5 oz (100 g): 1 skein #5101 Mochi (A)

Tools
D/3 (3.25 mm) crochet hook
E/4 (3.5 mm) crochet hook
yarn needle
rust-proof pins
one 2" x 2" (5 x 5 cm) piece of cardboard

Notes: All sts in Back and Fronts are worked in flo. All sts in Edgings are worked in both loops of sts.

BACK

With E/4 (3.5 mm) hook, ch 55 (57, 59).

Row 1: Working in back bump of ch sts, sc in 2nd ch from hook and in each of ch across, turn—54 (56, 58) sc.

Row 2: Ch 1, sc in each sc across, turn.

Row 3: Ch 1, 2 sc in first st, sc in the each st across to last 2 sts, 2 sc in next st, sc in last st, turn—56 (58, 60) sc.

Row 4–14 (16, 18): Rep Rows 2–3 [5 (6, 7) times], then rep Row 2 once—66 (70, 74) sc at end of last row.

Shape Armhole

Row 1: Ch 1, sc2tog over first 2 sts, sc in st across to last 2 sts, sc2tog in last 2 sts, turn—64 (68, 72) sts.

Row 2: Ch 1, sk first st, sc2tog in next 2 sts, sc in each st across to last 4 sts, sc2tog over next 2 sts, sk next st, sc in last st, turn—60 (64, 68) sts.

Row 3: Rep Row 2—56 (60, 64) sts.

Row 4: Ch 1, sc in each st across, turn.

Row 5: Rep Row 1—54 (58, 62) sts.

Row 6: Ch 1, sc in each st across, turn.

Row 7: Rep Row 1—52 (56, 60) sts.

Rows 8–19: Ch 1, sc in each st across, turn.

Row 20: Ch 1, 2 sc in first st, sc in the each st across to last 2 sts, 2 sc in next st, sc in last st, turn—54 (58, 62) sts.

Rows 21–25: Ch 1, sc in each st across, turn.

Row 26: Rep Row 20—56 (60, 64) sts.

Rows 27 (27–29, 27–31): Ch 1, sc in each st across, turn.

Left Shoulder Shaping

Row 1: Ch 1, sc in next 19 (20, 21) sts, sl st in next 2 sts, turn—21 (22, 23) sts.

Row 2: Ch 1, sk first 2 sts, sc in each st across, turn—19 (20, 21) sts.

Row 3: Ch 1, sc in each of the next 17 (18, 19) sts, sl st in last 2 sts, turn.

Row 4: Ch 1, sk first 2 sts, sc in next 15 (16, 17) sts, sl st in next st, 2 sl st in last st, turn—18 (19, 20) sts.

Row 5: Ch 1, sk first 2 sts, sc in next 15 (16, 17) sts, sl st in last st, turn—16 (17, 18) sts.

Row 6: Ch 1, sk first 2 sts, sc in each of st across, turn—14 (15, 16) sts.

Row 7: Ch 1, sl st in first 3 sts, sc in next 5 sts, hdc in next 4 (5, 6) sts, dc in last 2 sts—14 (15, 16) sts. Fasten off.

Right Shoulder Shaping

Row 1: Sk 14 (16, 18) sts from last st made in Row 1 of Left Shoulder Shaping, join yarn with sl st in next st, ch 1 (counts as a st), sl st in next 2 sts, sc in each st across, turn—21 (22, 23) sts.

Row 2: Ch 1, sc in first 17 (18, 19) sts, sl st in next 2 sts, turn—19 (20, 21) sts.

Row 3: Ch 1, sk first 2 sts, sc in each st across, turn—17 (18, 19) sts.

Row 4: Ch 1, 2 sl st in first st, sl st in next st, sc in next 13 (14, 15) sts, sl st in last 2 sts, turn—18 (19, 20) sts.

Row 5: Ch 1, sk first 2 sts, sc next 13 (14, 15) sts, sl st in last 3 sts, turn—16 (17, 18) sts.

Row 6: Ch 1, sk first 2 sts, sc in last 14 (15, 16) sts, turn—14 (15, 16) sts.

Row 7: Ch 3 (counts as dc), dc in next st, hdc in next 4 (5, 6) sts, sc in next 5 sts, sl st in last 3 sts. Fasten off—14 (15, 16) sts.

Neck Edging

Row 1: With right side of Back facing and E/4 (3.5 mm) hook, join yarn with a sl st in first row-end dc at end of Row 7 of Right Shoulder, ch 1, 2 sc in same row-end dc, sc in each row-end st along right neck edge, sc in each st across the bottom of the neckline, sc in each row-end st across left neck edge, 2 sc in last row-end dc at the shoulder. Fasten off.

Back Bottom Edging

Row 1: With right side of Back facing and bottom edge of Back on top, work over Row 1 of Back. Using an E/4 (3.5 mm) hook, join yarn with a sl st in first st in Row 2, yo and draw up a loop long enough to reach the edge of the Back, ch 1, working over the top edge of the back, sc in each st in Row 2 across, turn—54 (56, 58) sc.

Row 2: Ch 1, sl st in each st across—54 (56, 58) sl sts. Fasten off.

LEFT FRONT

With E/4 (3.5 mm), ch 19 (21, 23).

Row 1: Working in back bump of ch sts, sl st in 2nd ch from hook, sc in next 3 sts, hdc in next 13 (15, 17) ch, sc in last ch, turn—18 (19, 20) sts.

Row 2: Ch 1, sc in each st across to last 2 sts, 2 sc in next st, sc in last st, turn—19 (21, 23) sc.

Rows 3–5: Ch 1, sc in each st across, turn.

Row 6: Ch 1, sc in each st across to last st, 2 sc in last st, turn—20 (22, 24) sc.

Rows 7–10 (12, 14): Ch 1, sc in each st across, turn.

Shape Armhole

Row 1: Ch 1, sc in first 14 (15, 16) sts, turn, leaving rem sts unworked—14 (15, 16) sc.

Row 2: Ch 1, sk first st, sc in each st across to last 2 sts, sk next st, sc in last st, turn—12 (13, 14) sts.

Row 3: Ch 1, sc in each st across to last 2 sts, sk next st, sc in last st, turn—11 (12, 13) sts.

Row 4: Ch 1, sk first st, sc in each st across, turn—10 (11, 12) sts.

Row 5–8 (6, 7): Ch 1, sc in each st across, turn.

Row 9 (7, 8): Rep Row 2—8 (9, 10) sc.

Rows 10–12 (8–10, 9–12): Ch 1, sc in each st across, turn.

Row 13 (11, 13): Rep Row 2—6 (7, 8) sc.

Rows 14–19 (12–19, 14–19): Ch 1, sc in each st across, turn.

Row 20: Rep Row 4—5 (6, 7) sc.

Rows 21–25: Ch 1, sc in each st across, turn.

Fasten off, leaving a 5" (12.5 cm) sewing length.

RIGHT FRONT

With E/4 (3.5 mm), ch 19 (21, 23).

Row 1: Working in back bump of ch sts, sc in 2nd ch from hook, hdc in next 13 (15, 17) ch, sc in next 3 sts, sl st in last ch, turn—18 (19, 20) sts.

Row 2: Ch 1, sc in each st across to last 2 sts, 2 sc in next st, sc in last st, turn— 19 (21, 23) sc.

Rows 3–5: Ch 1, sc in each st across, turn.

Row 6: Ch 1, 2 sc in first sc, sc in each st across, turn—20 (22, 24) sc.

Rows 7–10 (12, 14): Ch 1, sc in each st across, turn.

Shape Armhole

Row 1: Ch 1, sl st in first 6 (7, 8) sts, sc in each rem st across, turn—14 (15, 16) sc.

Row 2: Ch 1, sk first st, sc in each st across to last 2 sc, sk next sc, sc in last sc, turn, leaving rem sl sts unworked—12 (13, 14) sc.

Row 3: Ch 1, sk first st, sc in each st across, turn—11 (12, 13) sts.

Row 4: Ch 1, sc in each st across to last 2 sts, sk next st, sc in last st, turn—10 (11, 12) sc.

Row 5–8 (6, 7): Ch 1, sc in each st across, turn.

Row 9 (7, 8): Rep Row 2—8 (9, 10) sc.

Rows 10–12 (8–10, 9–12): Ch 1, sc in each st across, turn.

Row 13 (11, 13): Rep Row 2—6 (7, 8) sc.

Rows 14–19 (12–19, 14–19): Ch 1, sc in each st across, turn.

Row 20: Rep Row 4—5 (6, 7) sc.

Rows 21–25: Ch 1, sc in each st across, turn.

Fasten off, leaving a 5" (12.5 cm) sewing length.

(continued)

Right Front Edging

Row 1: With right side of Right Front facing, work across opposite side of foundation ch, using E/4 (3.5 mm) hook, join yarn with a sl st in in first ch on bottom left-hand corner of bottom edge, ch 4 (counts as dc, ch 2), sk next ch, dc in next ch, *ch 2, sk next st, dc in next st; rep from * 6 (7, 8) times, working up front edge, ch 2, dc in first row-end st, **ch 2, sk next row, dc in next row-end st; rep from ** 16 (17, 18) times, turn—26 (28, 30) ch-2 sps.

Sizes 6 and 10 Only

Row 2: Ch 1, sc in first dc, 2 sc in next ch-2 sp, sc in next dc, ch 5, sc in next dc, 2 sc in next ch-2 sp, *sc in next dc, ch 4, sc in next dc, 2 sc in next ch-2 sp, sc in next dc, ch 5**, sc in next dc, 2 sc in ch-2 sp; rep from * across, ending last rep at **, sc in 2nd ch of the beg ch-4, turn—7 (8) ch-5 sps; 6 (7) ch-4 sps.

Row 3: Sl st in flo of first 3 ch sts in first ch-5 sp, ch 1, *sc in next ch-5 sp, ch 5**, (Cl, ch 5, Cl) in next ch-4 sp (shell made), ch 5; rep from * across, ending last rep at **, skip next 3 sc, sc in last sc, turn—7 (8) shells.

Row 4: Ch 7, sk next ch-5 sp, working over sc in Row 3, sc in next ch-5 sp 2 rows below, *ch 7, sc in next ch-5 sp of shell, ch 7, working over sc in Row 3, sc in next ch-5 sp 2 rows below; rep from * across—15 (17) ch-7 sps. Fasten off.

Size 8 Only

Row 2: Ch 1, sc in first dc, 2 sc in next ch-2 sp, *sc in next dc, ch 4, sc in next dc, 2 sc in next ch-2 sp, sc in next dc, ch 5**, sc in next dc, 2 sc in ch sp; rep from * across ending last rep at **, sc in 2nd ch of the beg ch-4, turn—7 ch-5 sps; 7 ch-4 sps.

Row 3: Sl st in flo of first 3 ch sts in first ch-5 sp, ch 1, *sc in next ch-5 sp, ch 5, (Cl, ch 5, Cl) in next ch-4 sp (shell made), ch 5; rep from * across to last ch-4 sp, skip next 3 sc, sc in last sc, turn—7 shells.

Row 4: *Ch 7, sk next ch-5 sp, sc in next ch-5 sp of shell, ch 7, working over sc in Row 3, sc in next ch-5 sp 2 rows below; rep from * across—14 ch-7 sps. Fasten off.

Left Front Edging

Row 1: With right side of Left Front facing, using E/4 (3.5 mm) hook, join yarn with a sl st in first ch on top right-hand corner of front edge, ch 4 (counts as dc, ch 2), sk next row, dc in next row-end st, *ch 2, sk next row, dc in next row-end st; rep from * 15 (16, 17) times, working across bottom edge of foundation ch, **ch 2, sk next ch, dc in next ch; rep from ** 8 (9, 10) times, turn—26 (28, 30) ch-2 sps.

Sizes 6 and 10 Only

Row 2: Ch 1, sc in first dc, *Ch 5, sc in next dc, 2 sc in next ch-2 sp**, sc in next dc, ch 4, sc in next dc, 2 sc in next ch-2 sp, sc in next dc; rep from * across, ending last rep at **, sc in 2nd ch of the beg ch-4, turn—7 (8) ch-5 sps; 6 (7) ch-4 sps.

Row 3: Ch 1, sc in first sc, *ch 5, sc in next ch-5 sp**, ch 5, (Cl, ch 5, Cl) in next ch-4 sp (shell made); rep from * across, ending last rep at **, turn.

Row 4: *Ch 7, sk next ch-5 sp, sc in next ch-5 sp of shell, ch 7, working over sc in Row 3, sc in next ch-5 sp 2 rows below; rep from * across to last ch-5 sp, ch 7, sk next ch-5 sp, sc in last sc. Fasten off.

Size 8 Only

Row 2: Ch 1, sc in first dc, *Ch 5, sc in next dc, 2 sc in next ch-2 sp, sc in next dc, ch 4, sc in next dc, 2 sc in next ch-2 sp, sc in next dc; rep from * across, ending with last sc in top of turning ch, turn—7 ch-5 sps; 7 ch-4 sps.

Row 3: Ch 1, sc in first sc, *ch 5, (Cl, ch 5, Cl) in next ch-4 sp (shell made), sc in next ch-5 sp**, ch 5; rep from * across, ending last rep at **, turn.

Row 4: *Ch 7, sk next ch-5 sp, sc in next ch-5 sp of shell**, ch 7, working over sc in Row 3, sc in next ch-5 sp 2 rows below; rep from * across, ending last rep at **, ch 7, sk next ch-5 sp, sc in last sc. Fasten off.

BLOCKING AND ASSEMBLY

Weave in ends. Pin out all pieces onto a blocking board and wet or steam block. When the pieces are dry, remove pins. Sew Fronts to Back at sides and shoulders.

LEFT ARMHOLE EDGING

Rnd 1: With right side facing, using E/4 (3.5 mm) hook, join yarn with a sl st in first st to the left of the underarm seam, ch 3 (counts as hdc, ch 1), [sk next st, hdc in next st, ch 1] 3 (3, 4) times, hdc in next row-end st, *ch 1, sk next row, hdc in next row-end st*; rep from * to * 11 times, ch 1, hdc in first row-end st of Back, rep from * to * 15 (14, 16) times, (ch 1, hdc) in each of next 4 (6, 4) row-end sts, ch 1, join with a sl st in 2nd ch of beg ch-3, turn. Invisible Fasten Off—37 (38, 39) ch-1 sps.

(continued)

Work now progresses in rows.

Row 2: With wrong side facing, using E/4 (3.5 mm) hook, join yarn with a sl st in 14th hdc below the shoulder seam, on the Back, ch 4, *sc in next hdc, sc in next ch-1 sp, sc in next hdc, ch 5, sc in next hdc, sc in next ch-1 sp, sc in next hdc, ch 4; rep from * 5 times, sc in next hdc, turn, leaving remaining sts unworked—6 ch-5 sps; 7 ch-4 sps.

Row 3: Ch 1, sc in next ch-4 sp, ch 5, *sc in next ch-5 sp, ch 4, (Cl, ch 5, Cl) in next ch-4 sp (shell made), ch 4; rep from * 4 times, sc in next ch-5 sp, ch 5, sc in last ch-4 sp, turn—5 shells.

Row 4: *[Ch 6, sk next ch-5 sp, working over sc in Row 3, sc in next ch-5 sp 2 rows below, ch 6, sk next ch-5 sp**, sc in next ch-5 sp of shell]* twice, [ch 7, sk next ch-5 sp, working over sc in Row 3, sc in next ch-5 sp 2 rows below, ch 6, sk next ch-5 sp**, sc in next ch-5 sp of shell] twice; rep from * to * once; rep from * to ** once, sl st in last sc in row—8 ch-6 sps; 4 ch-7 sps. Fasten off.

RIGHT ARMHOLE EDGING

Rnd 1: With right side facing, using E/4 (3.5 mm) hook, join yarn with a sl st in first st to the left of the underarm seam, ch 3 (counts as hdc, ch 1), sk next row-end st, (ch 1, hdc) in each of next 3 (4, 4) row-end sts, *ch 1, sk next row, hdc in next row-end st*; rep from * to * 13 (13, 15) times, ch 1, hdc in first row-end st of Front, rep from * to * 10 (10, 11) times, (ch 1, hdc) in each of next 4 (4, 2) row-end sts, [ch 1, sk next st, hdc in next st] 3 times, ch 1, join with a sl st in 2nd ch of beg ch-3, turn. Invisible Fasten Off—37 (38, 39) ch-1 sps.

Row 2: With wrong side facing, using E/4 (3.5 mm) hook, join yarn with a sl st in 12th hdc below the shoulder seam, on the Front, ch 4, *sc in next hdc, sc in next ch-1 sp, sc in next hdc, ch 5, sc in next hdc, sc in next ch-1 sp, sc in next hdc, ch 4; rep from * 5 times, sc in next hdc, turn, leaving remaining sts unworked—6 ch-5 sps; 7 ch-4 sps.

Rows 3–4: Rep Rows 3–4 of Left Armhole Edging.

TIES (MAKE 2)

With right side facing, using D/3 (3.25 mm) hook, join yarn in 6th (7th, 8th) sc from side seam on Right Front Edging, ch 72 (77, 82), working in back bar of ch sts, sl st in 6th ch from hook, sl st in each ch across. Fasten off. Starting in corresponding sc on Edging, rep Tie on Left Front.

TASSEL POPCORN (MAKE 2)

Wrap yarn twice around your finger to form an adjustable ring. Using E/4 (3.5 mm) hook, insert hook into ring, yo and pull up a lp, *ch 2, dc, tr, dc, hdc, sl st into ring, rep from * 3 times. Fasten off. Thread one Tassel Popcorn over each Tie and slide down temporarily.

Tassel

Thread a 95" (241 cm) length of yarn onto yarn needle. Take the ch-5 loop end of one Tie and place the loop at the top of the cardboard piece, *hold both while you pull the needle through the loop and wrap the yarn around the cardboard; rep from * until all yarn has been wrapped around cardboard. Cut a separate 12" (30.5 cm) length of yarn. Cut the wrapped loops across the bottom edge, and carefully remove the yarn from the cardboard. Wrap 12" (30.5 cm) strand of yarn around the Tassel several times, ⅝" (1.5 cm) from the folded end and tie securely. Slide the Tassel Popcorn down the Tie and over the top of the Tassel to cover the wrapped yarn. Pull on the tail end of the adjustable ring to tighten the Tassel Popcorn around the Tassel, tack in place so it does not move. Trim Tassel ends to same length. Rep Tassel on other Tie.

Finishing

Weave in ends. Pin the Top of Armhole Lace Edging out on a blocking board, and wet block. Spray the Tassel fringes with water, and lay them out straight to dry.

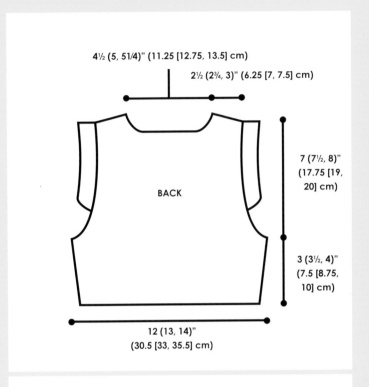

4½ (5, 5¼)" (11.25 [12.75, 13.5] cm)

2½ (2¾, 3)" (6.25 [7, 7.5] cm)

7 (7½, 8)" (17.75 [19, 20] cm)

BACK

3 (3½, 4)" (7.5 [8.75, 10] cm)

12 (13, 14)" (30.5 [33, 35.5] cm)

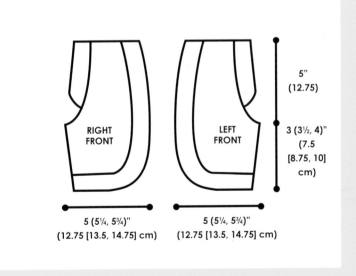

5" (12.75)

3 (3½, 4)" (7.5 [8.75, 10] cm)

RIGHT FRONT

LEFT FRONT

5 (5¼, 5¾)" (12.75 [13.5, 14.75] cm)

5 (5¼, 5¾)" (12.75 [13.5, 14.75] cm)

Sunny Day Skirt

This wrap skirt is made in three pieces, and is easy to construct and comfortable to wear. The nylon and acrylic blend yarn has a lovely softness that gives the crocheted fabric a wonderful drape. The eye-catching flower appliqué embellishments give this skirt a special touch that will have her standing out from the crowd with style.

Special Stitches Used

- **extended half double crochet (ehdc)**
  Yo, insert hook into indicated st and draw up a lp, yo, draw through first lp on hook, yo and draw through rem 3 lps on hook.

- **single crochet 2 together (sc2tog)**
  [Insert hook in next st, yo, draw yarn through st] twice, yo and draw through 3 lps on hook.

- **Invisible Fasten Off (page 14)**
  Cut yarn leaving a 3" (7.5 cm) tail. Insert hook in blo of first st in rnd, yo, and draw yarn all the way through the loop on the hook, as if to fasten off in the usual way. Insert the hook in both lps of next st, yo with tail end and pull through st. Finally, insert hook in flo of last st in rnd, yo, draw yarn down through.

- **2 double crochet cluster (2dcCL)**
  [Yo, insert hook in ring and draw up a lp, yo, draw yarn through 2 lps on hook] twice, yo, draw through 3 lps on hook.

- **3 double crochet cluster (3dcCL)**
  [Yo, insert hook in ring and draw up a lp, yo, draw yarn through 2 lps on hook] 3 times, yo, draw through 2 lps on hook, yo draw through 3 lps on hook.

- **2 treble crochet cluster (2trCL)**
  *Yo (twice), insert hook in ring and draw up a lp, [yo, draw through 2 lps on hook] twice, rep from * once, yo, draw through 3 lps on hook.

- **3 treble crochet cluster (3trCL)**
  *Yo (twice), insert hook in ring and draw up a lp, [yo, draw through 2 lps on hook] twice, rep from * twice, yo, draw through 4 lps on hook.

Skill Level
Advanced

Finished Size
Directions are given for girl's size 6. Changes for 8 and 10 are in parentheses.

Finished Waist: 23 (24, 25)" (58.5 [61, 63.5] cm)

Finished Hips: 26½ (27, 28)" (67.5 [68.5, 71] cm).

Finished Length: 15 (16, 17)" (38 [40.5, 43] cm).

Gauge
With E/4 (3.50 mm) hook, 20 sts and 13 rows in ehdc = 4" (10 cm)

Yarn

Berroco Comfort DK, 50% nylon, 50% acrylic; 1.75 oz (50 g)/178 yd (165 m): 3 (4, 4) skeins #2719 Sunshine (A) and 2 skeins #2706 Limone (B)

Tools
D/3 (3.25 mm) crochet hook

E/4 (3.50 mm) crochet hook

F/5 (3.75 mm) crochet hook

yarn needle

stitch markers

rust-proof pins

sewing needle

invisible nylon thread

BACK PANEL

With E/4 (3.50mm) hook and A, ch 60 (62, 64).

Row 1: Working in back bar of ch sts, ehdc in 3rd ch from hook and in each ch across, turn—58 (60, 62) ehdc. *Note: Ch 2 at beginning of each row does not count as a st, here and throughout.*

Row 2: Ch 2, ehdc in each st across, turn.

Row 3 (inc row): Ch 2, 2 ehdc in next st, ehdc in each st across to last 2 sts, 2 ehdc in next st, ehdc in last st, turn—62 (64, 66) ehdc.

Rows 4–11: Rep Row 2.

Row 12: Rep Row 3—64 (66, 68) ehdc.

Rows 13–14: Rep row 2.

Rows 15–44 (47, 50): Rep Rows 12–14 (10 [11, 13] times), increasing 2 sts at each end of next row and every 3rd row thereafter until 84 (88, 94) ehdc are on work.

Row 45 (48, 51): Rep Row 3—86 (90, 96) ehdc.

Rows 46–47 (49–50, 52–53): Ch 3 (counts as ehdc, ch 1 here and throughout), sk first st, ehdc in next st, *ch 1, sk next st, ehdc in next st, rep from * across, turn—43 (45, 48) ch-1 sps.

Row 48 (51, 54): Ch 2, 2 ehdc in next ch, ehdc in each st and sp across to last 2 sts, 2 ehdc in next ch, ehdc in last st, turn—87 (91, 95) ehdc. Fasten off.

SIDE FRONT PANEL

With E/4 (3.50mm) hook and A, ch 54 (55, 56).

Row 1: Working in back bar of ch sts, ehdc in 3rd ch from hook and in each ch across, turn—52 (53, 54) ehdc.

Row 2: Ch 2, ehdc in each st across, do not work in ch-2 turning ch, turn.

Row 3 (inc row): Ch 2, 2 ehdc in next st, ehdc in each st across, turn—53 (54, 55) ehdc.

The next 2 rows will vary depending upon whether the previous row has an odd or an even number of sts.

Row 4 (worked on an odd number of sts): Ch 2, ehdc in first st, *ch 1, sk next st, ehdc in next st, rep from * across, turn—26 (—, 27) ch-1 sps.

Row 4 (worked on an even number of sts): *Note: If there is an even number of sts in the previous row, there will be an extra st at the end of the row, work.* Ch 2, ehdc in first st, ehdc in next st, *ch 1, sk next st, ehdc in next st, rep from * across, turn— — (27, —) ch-1 sps.

Row 5 (worked on an odd number of sts): If there is an odd number of sts in the previous row, work: Ch 2, ehdc in first st, *ch 1, sk next st, ehdc in next st, rep from * across, turn—26 (—, 27) ch-1 sps.

Row 5 (worked on an even number of sts): If there is an even number of sts in the previous row, work the following: Ch 3 (counts as ehdc, ch 1), sk first st, ehdc in next ehdc, *ch 1, sk next ch-1 sp, ehdc in next ehdc, rep from * across, turn— —(27, —) ch-1 sps.

Row 6 (even): Rep Row 2—53 (54, 55) ehdc.

Row 7: Rep Row 5.

Row 8: Rep Row 4.

Rows 9 (even): Rep Row 2.

Rows 10–11: Rep Rows 4–5.

Note: All increases should be worked at left side edge of Panel. Place marker at the beginning of last row to mark left side edge for increases.

Row 12 (inc at end of row): Ch 2, ehdc in each st across to last 2 sts, 2 ehdc in next ch, ehdc in last ehdc, turn—54 (55, 56) ehdc.

Rows 13–14: Rep Rows 7–8.

Row 15 (inc at beg of row): Ch 2, 2 ehdc in next st, ehdc in each st across, turn—55 (56, 57) ehdc.

Rows 16–17: Rep Rows 4–5.

Row 18: Rep Row 12—56 (57, 58) ehdc.

Rows 19–48 (48, 54): Rep Rows 13–18 (5 [5, 6] times); then rep Rows 13–15 (0 [1, 0] times)—67 (68, 70) ehdc at end of last row. Fasten off.

SIDE FRONT EDGING

Row 1: With WS of Side Front Panel facing, beg at the top (at the waist) of the long straight edge, with E/4 (3.50 mm) hook, join A with a sl st in first row-end st, ch 2, hdc in first row-end st, 2 hdc in next row-end st, *ch 2, hdc between the 2 ch-sp rows, ch 2, 2 hdc in next row-end st of solid ehdc row, rep from * across, turn.

Row 2: Ch 2, hdc in next st, *hdc in next ch-2 sp, hdc in next hdc, hdc in next ch-2 sp, hdc next 2 hdc, rep from * across to last 2 sts, hdc in each of last 2 sts. Fasten off.

SIDE FRONT TIE

With D/3 (3.25 mm) hook and A, ch 96 (98, 100).

Row 1: Working in back bar of ch sts, sc in 2nd ch from hook and in each ch across, turn—95 (97, 99) sc. Change to B.

Row 2: With B, sk first st, sc in each rem st across, turn—94 (96, 98) sc. Change to A.

Row 3: With A, ch 1, sc in each st across, turn. Change to B.

Row 4: Rep Row 2—93 (95, 97) sc. Change to A.

Row 5: With A, ch 1, sc in each st across to last 2 sts, sc2tog over last 2 sts—92 (94, 96) sts. Fasten Off.

FRONT PANEL TIE

With D/3 (3.25 mm) hook and A, ch 152 (156, 160).

Rows 1–5: Work same as Rows 1–5 of Side Front Tie—148 (152, 156) sts at end of last row). Fasten off.

BELT LOOPS (MAKE 2)

With D/3 (3.25 mm) hook and A, ch 10.

Rnd 1: Working in blo of ch sts, sc in 2nd ch from hook and in each ch across, turn to work across rem front loops of foundation ch, sc in rem front lp of each st across. Invisible Fasten off.

(continued)

FRONT PANEL APPLIQUÉS

Small Flower

With E/4 (3.50 mm) hook and A, make a Magic Ring (see page 15).

Rnd 1: Yo and draw up a lp, ch 3, 2dcCL in ring, *ch 11 (12, 12), 3dcCL in ring, rep from * 4 times, ch 11 (12, 12), sl st in top of beg 2dcCl. Pull on tail end of yarn to close ring.

Rnd 2: *Sl st in blo of each of the next 11 (12, 12) ch sts, sl st in both lps of cluster, rep from * around. Fasten off.

Medium Flower

With E/4 (3.50 mm) hook and A, make a Magic Ring.

Rnd 1: Yo and draw up a lp, ch 3, 2dcCL in ring, *ch 17 (18, 18), 3dcCL in ring, rep from * 4 times, ch 17 (18, 18), sl st in top of beg 2dcCL. Pull on tail end of yarn to close ring.

Rnd 2: *Sl st in blo of each of the next 17 (18, 18) ch sts, sl st in both lps of next CL, rep from * around. Fasten off.

Large Flower

With E/4 (3.50 mm) hook and A, make a Magic Ring.

Rnd 1: Yo and draw up a lp, ch 4, 2trCL in ring, *ch 19 (20, 20), 3trCL in ring, rep from * 6 times, ch 19 (20, 20), sl st in top of beg 2trCl. Pull on tail end of yarn to close ring.

Rnd 2: *Sl st in blo of each of the next 19 (20, 20) ch sts, sl st in both lps of next CL, rep from * around. Fasten off.

Small Dots (Make 3)

With E/4 (3.50 mm) hook and A, make a Magic Ring.

Rnd 1: Yo and pull up a lp, ch 2, work 9 hdc in ring—10 hdc. Pull on tail end of yarn to close ring. Invisible Fasten Off.

Medium Dots (Make 4)

With E/4 (3.50 mm) hook and A, make a Magic Ring.

Rnd 1: Yo and pull up a lp, ch 3, work 9 dc in ring—10 dc. Pull on tail end of yarn to close ring. Invisible Fasten Off.

Large Dots (Make 2)

With E/4 (3.50 mm) hook and A, make a Magic Ring.

Rnd 1: Yo and pull up a lp, ch 2, work 8 sc in ring. Sl st in beg sc to end rnd. Pull on tail end of yarn to close ring.

Rnd 2: Ch 3, dc in same st, 2 dc in each st around—18 dc. Invisible Fasten Off.

Embellish all of the dots in the following manner. Using a yarn needle and B, come up in the center of a Dot and go down in a st at the outside edge. Repeat around the surface of the dot in every other st around.

ASSEMBLY

Pin out all pieces on a blocking board and wet or steam block. Sew the right side of the Front Panel to the left side of the Back Panel, then sew the right side of the Back Panel to the left side of the Side Front Panel from the bottom to the top, stopping 3 rows from the top, sk 2 rows to leave an opening for the Tie, then st the top rows of each panel together.

SURFACE CROCHET TRIM

Use F/5 (3.75 mm) hook and B to work surface crochet on top of Rows 45 and 48 (48 and 51, 51 and 54) beg on the Side Front Panel and continuing across the Back Panel. With the side edge of the Side Front Panel facing you, insert your hook between the first and second st of one of the indicated rows, keeping the yarn underneath the work, yo and draw up a lp, *insert hook between next 2 sts in the row, yo and draw up a lp, ch 1,

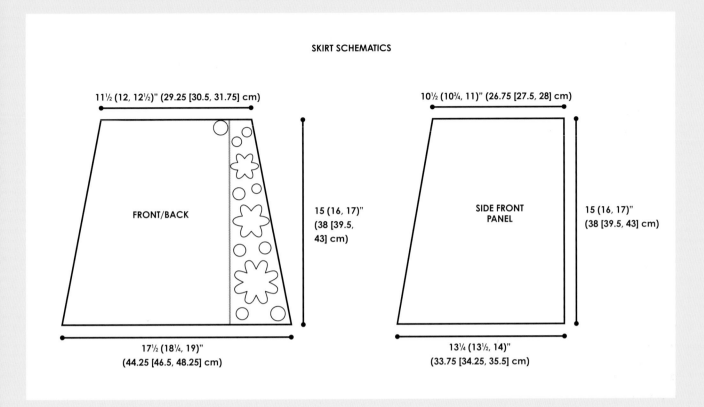

SKIRT SCHEMATICS

11½ (12, 12½)" (29.25 [30.5, 31.75] cm)

FRONT/BACK

15 (16, 17)" (38 [39.5, 43] cm)

17½ (18¼, 19)" (44.25 [46.5, 48.25] cm)

10½ (10¾, 11)" (26.75 [27.5, 28] cm)

SIDE FRONT PANEL

15 (16, 17)" (38 [39.5, 43] cm)

13¼ (13½, 14)" (33.75 [34.25, 35.5] cm)

rep from * across Side Front Panel and Back Panel. When you get to the last st of the back panel, remove lp from hook, insert hook between the Front Panel and Back Panel from the bottom of the work to the top, and pull last lp to the bottom of the work. Fasten off. Rep these instructions on other indicated row.

SIDE FRONT, BACK AND FRONT PANEL EDGING

With E/4 (3.50 mm) hook, with the (RS) facing, join B with a sl st in bottom right-hand corner of Side Front Panel, working between the sts, sc between the first and second st, *sk sp between the next 2 sts, sc in next sp bet sts*, rep from * to * across to top edge of this panel. **Note:** *For sizes 6 and 10, you will have only one st rem at the end of this side, so you will not sk a space, the corner will be in the next space.* Work 2 more sc in the corner, rep from * to * across top edge of all 3 panels, sk first Row of the Side Panel Edging, then, make 2 sc between this first Row and the first and second

sts of the Side Front Panel. *Sk the sp between the next 2 sts, sc between the foll 2 sts*. Rep from * to * across the top of all 3 panels, sc in the sp between the last 2 sts of the Front Panel. Fasten off.

FINISHING

Sew Front Panel Tie to the top left-hand side of the Front Panel, one row down from the top (not including the edging). Sew Side Front Panel Tie to the top right-hand side of the Side Front Panel, placing it ¼" (6 mm) below the panel edging.

Sew one Belt Loop 3¾" (8.25 cm) from each side of the Back Panel, beg one row down from the top (not including the edging).

Sew the Flowers and Dots to the Front Panel with a sewing needle and invisible nylon thread, following Assembly Diagram. Sew last Large Dot to the top right corner of the Side Front Panel.

Weave in ends.

Chelsea Capelet

When the weather is a little chilly, this capelet is an ideal fashionable layering piece. It is a great alternative to a poncho, allowing more freedom of movement so she can be active when she is on the go. For a different look, skip the flower embellishments and make a color blocked version, crocheting the center section of the front, the back, and cowl neck in other colors.

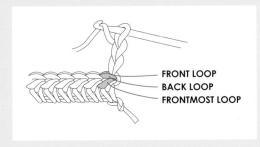

FRONT LOOP
BACK LOOP
FRONTMOST LOOP

Special Stitches Used

- **short single crochet (ssc)**
  Insert hook in the front-most horizontal lp (below top 2 lps) of next st, yo, draw yarn through st, yo, draw yarn through 2 lps on the hook.

- **short half double crochet (shdc)**
  Yo, insert hook in the front-most horizontal lp (below top 2 lps) of next st, yo, draw yarn through st, yo, draw yarn through 3 lps on the hook.

- **short double crochet (sdc)**
  Yo, insert hook in the front-most horizontal lp (below top 2 lps) of next st, yo, draw yarn through st, [yo, draw yarn through 2 lps on the hook] twice.

- **back post half double crochet (BPhdc)**
  Yo, insert hook from back to front to back again around the post of next st, yo, draw yarn through, yo, draw yarn through 3 lps on the hook.

- **Invisible Fasten Off (page 14)**
  Cut yarn leaving a 3" (7.5 cm) tail. Insert hook in blo of first st in rnd, yo, and draw yarn all the way through the loop on the hook, as if to fasten off in the usual way. Insert the hook in both lps of next st, yo with tail end and pull through st. Finally, insert hook in flo of last st in rnd, yo, draw yarn down through.

Skill Level
Intermediate

Finished Size
Directions are given for girl's size 6. Changes for 8 and 10 are in parentheses.

Finished Chest: 27 (29, 31)" (68.5 [73.5, 79] cm)

Finished Length: 10½ (11½, 13)" (26.5 [29, 33] cm)

Gauge
17 sts and 14 rows in Back pattern (alternating 1 row hdc and 1 row of shdc) = 4" (10 cm)

Yarn

3

Universal Yarn Uptown DK, 100% acrylic, 273 yd (250 m)/ 3.5 oz (100 g): 2 (2, 3) skeins #104 Bashful

Tools
G/6 (4mm) crochet hook

yarn needle

rust-proof pins

BACK

Ch 66 (70, 74).

Row 1: Working in back bar of ch sts, hdc in 3rd ch from the hook, hdc in each ch across, turn—64 (68, 72) hdc. ***Note:*** Ch 2 at beginning of row does not count as a st.

Row 2: Ch 2 (does not count as a st here and throughout), hdc in each st across, turn.

Row 3 (dec row): Ch 2, sk first st, hdc in each st across to last 2 sts, sk next st, hdc in last st, turn—62 (66, 70) sts.

Row 4: Ch 2, hdc in flo of first st, shdc in each st across to last st, hdc in flo of last st, turn.

Row 5: Ch 2, hdc in each st across, turn.

Row 6: Rep Row 4.

Rows 7–9: Rep Rows 3–5—60 (64, 68) sts.

Row 10: Rep Row 4.

Rows 11–13: Rep Rows 3–5—58 (62, 66) sts.

Sizes 8 and 10 Only

Rows 14–15 (17): Rep Rows 4–5 (1 [2]) times.

Shape Armhole (all sizes)

Row 14 (16, 18): Sl st in first 3 sts, ssc in next st, shdc in each of next 50 (54, 58) sts, ssc in next st, sl st in next st, turn— 52 (56, 60) sts.

Row 15 (17, 19): Ch 2, sk first sl st, hdc in each of the next 50 (54, 58) sts, sk next st, hdc in next st, turn—51 (55, 59) sts.

Rows 16–33 (18–37, 20–41): Rep Rows 4–5 (9 [10, 11]) times.

Shape Left Neck and Shoulder

Row 34 (38, 42): Ch 2, hdc in flo of the first st, shdc in next 17 (18, 19) sts, sk next st, shdc in next st, turn—19 (20, 21) sts.

Row 35 (39, 43): Ch 2, sk first st, hdc in each st across, turn—18 (19, 20) sts.

Row 36 (40, 44): Sc in flo of first st, ssc in next 5 sts, shdc in next 10 (11, 12) sts, sk next st, shdc in last st, turn—17 (18, 19) sts.

Row 37 (41, 45): Ch 3 (counts as dc), dc in first st, hdc in next 10 (11, 12) sts, sc in each of next 2 sts, sl st in next st—15 (16, 17) sts. Fasten off.

Shape Right Neck and Shoulder

Row 34 (38, 42): With WS facing, sk next 11 (13, 15) sts to the left of last st made in first row of Left Neck, join yarn with a sl st in next st, ch 2, sk first st, shdc in next 18 (19, 20) sts, hdc in the flo of the last st, turn—19 (20, 21) sts.

Row 35 (39, 43): Ch 2, hdc in first 17 (18, 19) sts, sk next st, hdc in last st, turn— 18 (19, 20) sts.

Row 36 (40, 44): Ch 2, sk first st, shdc in next 11 (12, 13) sts, ssc in next 5 sts, sc in flo of last st, turn—17 (18, 19) sts.

Row 37 (41, 45): Sl st in first 3 sts, sc in next 2 sts, hdc in next 10 (11, 12) sts, dc in last 2 sts—17 (18, 19) sts. Fasten off.

FRONT

Ch 66 (70, 74).

Row 1: Working in back bar of ch sts, hdc in 3rd ch from the hook, hdc in each ch across, turn—64 (68, 72) hdc.

Row 2: Ch 2, hdc in first 21 (23, 25) sts, ch 2, sk next 2 sts, hdc in blo of next 18 sts, ch 2, sk next 2 sts, hdc in last 21 (23, 25) sts, turn.

Row 3: Ch 2, sk first st, hdc in next 20 (22, 24) sts, 2 hdc in next ch-2 sp, hdc in blo of next 18 sts, 2 hdc in next ch-2 sp, hdc in next 19 (21, 23) sts, sk next st, hdc in last st, turn—62 (66, 70) sts.

Row 4: Ch 2, hdc in flo of first st, shdc in next 19 (21, 23) sts, ch 2, sk next 2 sts, hdc in blo of next 18 sts, ch 2, sk next 2 sts, shdc in next 19 (21, 23) sts, hdc in flo of last st, turn.

Row 5: Ch 2, hdc in first 20 (22, 24) sts, 2 hdc in next ch-2 sp, hdc in blo of next 18 sts, 2 hdc in next ch-2 sp, hdc in last 20 (22, 24) sts, turn.

Row 6: Rep Row 4.

Row 7: Ch 2, sk first st, hdc in next 19 (21, 23) sts, 2 hdc in next ch-2 sp, hdc in blo of next 18 sts, 2 hdc in next ch-2 sp, hdc in next 18 (20, 22) sts, sk next st, hdc in last st, turn—60 (64, 68) sts.

Row 8: Ch 2, hdc in flo of first st, shdc in next 18 (20, 22) sts, ch 2, sk next 2 sts, hdc in blo of next 18 sts, ch 2, sk next 2 sts, shdc in next 18 (20, 22) sts, hdc in flo of last st, turn.

Row 9: Ch 2, hdc in first 19 (21, 23) sts, 2 hdc in next ch-2 sp, hdc in blo of next 18 sts, 2 hdc in next ch-2 sp, hdc in last 19 (21, 23) sts, turn.

Row 10: Rep Row 8.

Row 11: Ch 2, sk first st, hdc in each of the next 18 (20, 22) sts, 2 hdc in next ch-2 sp, hdc in blo of next 18 sts, 2 hdc in next ch-2 sp, hdc in next 17 (19, 21) sts, sk next st, hdc in last st, turn—58 (62, 66) sts.

Row 12: Ch 2, hdc in flo of first st, shdc in next 17 (19, 21) sts, ch 2, sk next 2 sts, hdc in blo of next 18 sts, ch 2, sk next 2 sts, shdc in next 17 (19, 21) sts, hdc in flo of last st, turn.

Row 13: Ch 2, hdc in first 18 (20, 22) sts, 2 hdc in next ch-2 sp, hdc in blo of next 18 sts, 2 hdc in next ch-2 sp, hdc in last sts, turn—18 (20, 22) sts.

Sizes 8 and 10 Only

Rows 14–15 (14–17): Rep Rows 12–13 (1 [2] times).

Shape Armhole (all sizes)

Row 14 (16, 18): Sl st in first 2 sts, sl st in flo of next st, ssc in next st, shdc in each of the next 14 (16, 18) sts, ch 2, sk next 2 sts, hdc in blo of next 18 sts, ch 2, sk next 2 sts, shdc in next 14 (16, 18) sts, ssc in next st, sl st in flo of next st, turn—56 (60, 64) sts.

Row 15 (17, 19): Ch 2, sk first st, hdc in next 15 (17, 19) sts, 2 hdc in next ch-2 sp, hdc in blo of next 18 sts, 2 hdc in next ch-2 sp, hdc in next 14 (16, 18) sts, sk next st, hdc in last st, turn—52 (56, 60) sts.

Row 16 (18, 20): Ch 2, sk first st, shdc in next 14 (16, 18) sts, ch 2, sk next 2 sts, hdc in blo of next 18 sts, ch 2, sk next 2 sts, shdc in next 13 (15, 17) sts, sk next st, hdc in flo of last st, turn—50 (54, 58) sts.

Row 17 (19, 21): Ch 2, sk first st, hdc in next 13 (15, 17) sts, 2 hdc in next ch-2 sp, hdc in blo of the next 18 sts, 2 hdc in next ch-2 sp, hdc in next 12 (14, 16) sts, sk next st, hdc in last, turn—48 (52, 56) sts.

Row 18 (20, 22): Ch 2, sk first st, shdc in next 12 (14, 16) sts, ch 2, sk next 2 sts, hdc in blo of next 18 sts, ch 2, sk next 2 sts, shdc in next 11 (13, 15) sts, sk next st, hdc in flo of last st, turn—46 (50, 54) sts.

Row 19 (21, 23): Ch 2, sk first st, hdc in next 11 (13, 15) sts, 2 hdc in next ch-2 sp, hdc in blo of next 18 sts, 2 hdc in next ch-2 sp, hdc in next 10 (12, 14) sts, sk next st, hdc in last st, turn—44 (48, 52) sts.

Row 20 (22, 24): Ch 2, hdc in flo of first st, shdc in next 10 (12, 14) sts, ch 2, sk next 2 sts, hdc in blo of next 18 sts, ch 2, sk next 2 sts, shdc in next 10 (12, 14) sts, hdc in flo of last st, turn.

Row 21 (23, 25): Ch 2, hdc in the first 11 (13, 15) sts, 2 hdc in next ch-2 sp, hdc in blo of next 18 sts, 2 hdc in next ch-2 sp, hdc in last 11 (13, 15) sts, turn.

Rows 22–25 (24–27, 26–29): Rep last 2 rows twice.

(continued)

Shape Right Neck and Shoulder

Row 26 (28, 30): Ch 2, sk first st, shdc in the next 10 (12, 14) sts, ch 2, sk next 2 sts, hdc in blo of the next 5 sts, sl st in the the next st, turn—18 (20, 22) sts.

Row 27 (29, 31): Ch 2, sk the first sl st, hdc in blo of the next 5 sts, 2 hdc in the ch sp, hdc in last 10 (12, 14) sts, turn—17 (19, 21) sts.

Row 28 (30, 32): Ch 2, hdc in flo of first st, shdc in the next 9 (11, 13) sts, ch 2, sk 2 sts, hdc in blo of the next 3 sts, sk the next st, hdc in last st, turn—16 (18, 20) sts.

Row 29 (31, 33): Ch 2, sk the first st, hdc in blo of the first 3 sts, 2 hdc in the ch sp, hdc in last 10 (12, 14) sts, turn—15 (17, 19) sts.

Row 30 (32, 34): Ch 2, hdc in flo of first st, shdc in the next 9 (11, 13) sts, ch 2, sk 2 sts, hdc in blo of the last 3 sts, turn.

Row 31 (33, 35): Ch 2, hdc in blo of the first 3 sts, 2 hdc in the ch sp, hdc in last 10 (12, 14) sts, turn.

Rows 32–34 (34–36, 36–38): Rep last 2 rows once, then rep Row 30 (32, 34) once.

Row 35 (37, 39): Ch 2, hdc in blo of the first 3 sts, 2 hdc in the ch sp, hdc in next 9 (11, 13) sts, 2 hdc in last st, turn—16 (18, 20) sts.

Sizes 8 and 10 Only

Row 38 (40): Ch 2, hdc in flo of first st, shdc in the next 12 (14) sts, ch 2, sk next 2 sts, hdc in blo of the last 3 sts, turn.

Row 39 (41): Ch 2, hdc in blo of the first 3 sts, 2 hdc in next ch-2 sp, hdc in last 13 (15) sts, turn.

Size 10 Only

Rows 42–43: Rep last 2 rows.

All Sizes

Row 36 (40, 44): Ch 1, sc in flo of the first st, ssc in next 4 (5, 6) sts, shdc in next 10 (11, 12) sts, sdc in last st. Fasten off, leaving a 10" (25 cm) sewing length.

Shape Left Neck and Shoulder

Row 26 (28, 30): With WS facing, sk next 6 sts to the left of last st made in first row of Right Neck, join yarn in next st, ch 2 (does not count as a st), hdc in blo of same st, hdc in blo of next 5 sts, ch 2, sk next 2 sts, shdc in the next 9 (11, 13) sts, sk next st, hdc in the flo of last st, turn—17 (19, 21) sts.

Row 27 (29, 31): Ch 2, hdc in first 10 (12, 14) sts, 2 hdc in next ch-2 sp, hdc in blo of the next 5 sts, turn—17 (19, 21) sts.

Row 28 (30, 32): Ch 2, sk the first st, hdc in blo of next 4 sts, ch 2, sk 2 sts, shdc in next 9 (11, 13) sts, hdc in flo of the last st, turn—16 (18, 20) sts.

Row 29 (31, 33): Ch 2, hdc in first 10 (12, 14) sts, 2 hdc in next ch-2 sp, hdc in blo of next 2 sts, sk next st, hdc in blo of last st, turn—15 (17, 19) sts.

Row 30 (32, 34): Ch 2, hdc in blo of first 3 sts, ch 2, sk next 2 sts, shdc in next 9 (11, 13) sts, hdc in flo of last st, turn.

Row 31 (33, 35): Ch 2, hdc in first 10 (12, 14) sts, 2 hdc in next ch-2 sp, hdc in blo of last 3 sts, turn.

Row 32–34 (34–36, 36–38): Rep last 2 rows once, then rep Row 31 (33, 35) once.

Row 35 (37, 39): Ch 2, 2 hdc in the first st, hdc in the next 9 (11, 13) sts, 2 hdc in the ch sp, hdc in blo of the last 3 sts, turn—16 (18, 20) sts.

Sizes 8 and 10 Only

Row 38 (40): Ch 2, hdc in blo of first 3 sts, ch 2, sk 2 sts, shdc in the next 12 (14) sts, hdc in the flo of the last st, turn.

Row 39 (41): Ch 2, hdc in the first 13 (15) sts, 2 hdc in the ch-2 sp, hdc in blo of the last 3 sts, turn.

Size 10 Only

Row 42–43: Rep last 2 rows.

All Sizes

Row 36 (40, 44): Ch 3, dc in flo of the first st, shdc in next 10 (11, 12) sts, ssc in next 4 (5, 6), sc in flo of the last st. Fasten off, leaving a 10" (25 cm) sewing length.

ASSEMBLY

Pin Back and Front pieces on a blocking board and wet or steam block. Sew Front and Back together at shoulders and sides to armhole.

(continued)

ARMHOLE EDGING

Rnd 1: With RS facing, join yarn in first st to the left of side seam in one underarm, ch 1, sc in each st and row-end st around, join with a sl st in first sc, turn.

Rnd 2: Ch 2, BPhdc in each st around. Invisible Fasten Off.

COWL NECK

Rnd 1: With G/6 (4mm) hook, join yarn with a sl st in left front shoulder seam on neck edge, ch 1, sc in seam, sc in each of next 11 (13, 15) row-end sts, sc in next 6 sts, sc in each of next 11 (13, 15) row-end sts, sc in the shoulder seam, sc in each of next 4 row-end sts, sc in next 11 (13, 15) sts, s c in each of next 4 row-end sts, join with a sl st in first sc, turn—49 (55, 59) sts.

Rnd 2: 2 sc in same st, *ch 2, sk 2 sts, 2 sc in next st, rep from * 16 (18, 19) times, ch 2, join with a sl st between first 2 sc at beg of rnd—72 (80, 84) sts.

Rnd 3: 2 sc in same sp (between first 2 sc), *ch 2, sk next ch-2 sp, 2 sc in next sc, rep from * 16 (18, 19) times, ch 2, join with a sl st between first 2 sc at beg of rnd.

Rnds 4–6: 2 sc in same st (between first 2 sc), *ch 3, sk next ch-2 sp, 2 sc in next sc, rep from * 16 (18, 19) times, ch 3, join with a sl st between first 2 sc at beg of rnd.

Rnds 7–9: 2 sc in same st (between first 2 sc), *ch 4, sk next ch-2 sp, 2 sc in next sc, rep from * 16 (18, 19) times, ch 4, join with a sl st between first 2 sc at beg of rnd.

Rnds 10–26: 2 sc in same st (between first 2 sc), *ch 5, sk next ch-2 sp, 2 sc in next sc, rep from * 16 (18, 19) times, ch 5, join with a sl st between first 2 sc at beg of rnd.

Note: To make a bold edging, the sts in Rnd 27 will be worked over the ch-5 lps in last 2 rnds as if they were one lp.

Rnd 27: *Work 6 hdc over next 2 ch-5 lps in previous 2 rows, sl st between next 2 sc, rep from * around. Fasten off.

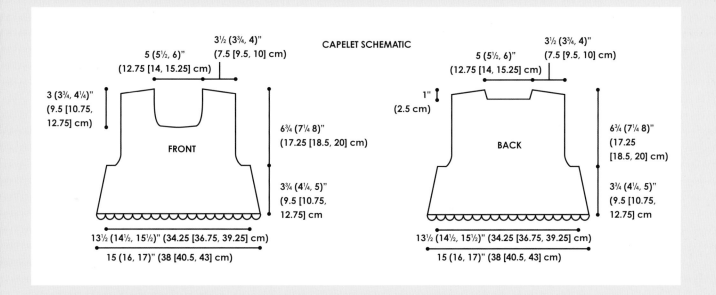

CAPELET SCHEMATIC

FRONT

3 (3¾, 4¼)" (9.5 [10.75, 12.75] cm)

5 (5½, 6)" (12.75 [14, 15.25] cm)

3½ (3¾, 4)" (7.5 [9.5, 10] cm)

6¾ (7¼ 8)" (17.25 [18.5, 20] cm)

3¾ (4¼, 5)" (9.5 [10.75, 12.75] cm

13½ (14½, 15½)" (34.25 [36.75, 39.25] cm)

15 (16, 17)" (38 [40.5, 43] cm)

BACK

5 (5½, 6)" (12.75 [14, 15.25] cm)

3½ (3¾, 4)" (7.5 [9.5, 10] cm)

1" (2.5 cm)

6¾ (7¼ 8)" (17.25 [18.5, 20] cm)

3¾ (4¼, 5)" (9.5 [10.75, 12.75] cm

13½ (14½, 15½)" (34.25 [36.75, 39.25] cm)

15 (16, 17)" (38 [40.5, 43] cm)

BOTTOM EDGING

Rnd 1: With RS facing, working across opposite side of foundation ch on bottom edge of capelet, join yarn with a sl st in first ch to the left of right side seam, ch 5 (counts as dc, ch 2), sk next 2 sts, *dc in each of next 2 sts, ch 2, sk next 2 sts, rep from * around, ending with dc in last st, join with a sl st in in 3rd ch of beg ch-5—32 (34, 36) ch-2 sps.

Rnd 2: *Ch 6, sk next ch-2 sp, sc between next 2 dc, rep from * around, ending with last sc between last dc and beg ch-3, join with a sl st in first ch of beg ch-6—32 (34, 36) ch-6 sps.

Rnd 3: *Work 6 sc in next ch-6 sp, sc in next sc, rep from * to * around—224 (238, 252) sc. Invisible Fasten Off.

FLOWERS

Bottom (Make 2)

Make a Magic Ring.

Rnd 1: Yo and draw up a lp, *ch 14 (15, 15), sl st in ring, rep from * 6 times. Pull on tail end of yarn to close ring.

Rnd 2: *Work 19 (20, 20) hdc in next ch-lp, sl st between this lp and next lp, rep from * around. Fasten off.

Middle (Make 2)

Make a Magic Ring.

Rnd 1: Yo and draw up a lp, *ch 12 (13, 13), sl st in ring, rep from * 4 times. Pull on tail end of yarn to close ring.

Rnd 2: *Work 17 (18, 18) hdc in next ch-lp, sl st between this lp and next lp, rep from * around. Fasten off.

Top (Make 2)

Make a Magic Ring.

Rnd 1: Yo and draw up a lp, *ch 9 (10, 10), sl st in ring, rep from * twice. Pull on tail end of yarn to close ring.

Rnd 2: *Work 14 (15, 15) sc in next ch-lp, sl st between this lp and next lp, rep from * around. Fasten off.

FINISHING

Weave in ends. Block capelet, paying special attention to the Cowl Neck and the Bottom Edging. Stack the bottom, middle, and top flower piece together for each Flower and sew together in the center. Sew top Flower in the middle of the front 2¼ (2½, 3)" (5.5 [6.5, 7.5] cm) below base of Cowl Neck. Sew bottom flower 3½" (9 cm) below top Flower.

Hip to Be Me Vest

She'll own her style in this rockin' vest. It's hip to be one of a kind, just like her. The integrated fringe offers just enough flair to make this vest "edgy" without going over the edge. When you make this trendy vest in affordable yarns, you can afford to make one for each member of her troupe of friends.

Skill Level
Easy

Finished Size
Directions are given for girl's size 4. Changes for 6, 8, 10, and 12 are in parentheses.
Finished Chest: 24½ (25½, 29, 30, 32½)" (62 [65, 73.5, 76, 82.5] cm)
Finished Length: 14 (15, 16½, 17½, 19)" (35.5 [38, 42, 44.5, 48.5] cm)

Gauge
14 sts and first 9 rows in Vest patt = 4" (10 cm). Take time to check gauge.

Yarn

Red Heart Sport, 100% acrylic, 2.5 oz (70 g)/165 yds (151 m) per skein: 1 (1, 1, 2, 2) skeins #0585 Purple (A), 1 skein each of #0652 Limeade (B), #0819 Blue Jewel (C) and #0846 Skipper Blue (D)

Tools
I/9 (5.5 mm) crochet hook
yarn needle
stitch markers

Notes: The foundation chain rests at the shoulders. Stitches are worked down from the foundation chain to make the back. The unused loops of the foundation chain will be used again and stitches worked down to make the fronts of the vest. Side seams are joined and edging added.

COLOR SEQUENCE

Work all pieces in the following color sequence: *2 rows A, 2 rows B, 2 rows C, 2 rows D, rep from * throughout.

BACK

With A, ch 37 (39, 41, 43, 45).

Row 1 (RS): Dc in 4th ch from hook and in each ch across, turn—35 (37, 39, 41, 43) dc.

Row 2 (WS): Ch 4 (counts as dc, ch 1), sk first 2 sts, *dc in next st, ch 1, sk next st, rep from * across to last st, dc in last st, turn—17 (18, 19, 20, 21) ch-1 sps.

Row 3: Ch 1, sc in first st, *working behind ch-1 sp, dc in skipped dc 2 rows below, sc in next dc; rep from * across, turn—35 (37, 39, 41, 43) sts.

Row 4: Ch 4 (counts as dc, ch 1), sk first 2 sts, *dc in next st, ch 1, sk next st, rep from * across to last st, dc in last st, turn.

Row 5: Ch 3 (counts as dc here and throughout), dc in each st and sp across, turn—35 (37, 39, 41, 43) dc.

Rep Rows 2–5 for pat, working increases as indicated.

Shape Armhole

Row 6: Rep Row 2.

Row 7 (Row 3 with inc): Ch 1, 2 sc in first st (inc made), *working behind ch-1 sp, dc in skipped dc 2 rows below, sc in next dc, rep from * across, ending with 2 sc in the last st (inc made), turn—37 (39, 41, 43, 45) sts.

Row 8: Rep Row 4 (no inc).

Row 9 (Row 5 with inc): Ch 3, 2 dc in same st (2 inc made), dc in each st and sp across, 3 dc in last st (2 inc made), turn—41 (43, 45, 47, 49) st.

Rows 10–11 (11, 13, 13, 15): Rep Rows 6–9 (0 [0, 1, 1, 1]) times, then rep Rows 6–7 (1 [1, 0, 0, 0, 1]) time—43 (45, 51, 53, 57) sts at end of last row.

Rows 12–31 (12–33, 14–37, 14–29, 16–43): Starting with Row 4 (4, 2, 2, 4), maintaining color sequence, work even in established patt, with no increases for 20 (22, 24, 26, 28) rows or for desired length. Fasten off.

RIGHT FRONT

Row 1 (RS): With RS facing, working across opposite side of foundation ch, join A with a sl st in first ch, ch 3, dc in each of next 8 (10, 10, 10, 10) ch sts, turn, leaving rem sts unworked—9 (11, 11, 11, 11) dc.

Rows 2–31 (33, 37, 29, 43): Work same as back, working increases on both sides for armhole and front neck shaping—17 (19, 23, 23, 25) sts at widest. Fasten off.

LEFT FRONT

With RS facing, working across opposite side of foundation ch, sk 17 (15, 17, 19, 21) ch sts at center back neck, join A with a sl st in next ch, dc in each ch across, turn—9 (11, 11, 11, 11) dc.

Rows 2–31 (33, 37, 29, 43): Work same as back, working increases on both sides for armhole and front neck shaping—17 (19, 23, 23, 25) sts at widest. Fasten off.

Block vest.

ASSEMBLY

With RS of front and back facing, using yarn needle and A, whipstitch side seam from bottom hem up to end of armhole shaping. Repeat for opposite side seam.

Weave in ends.

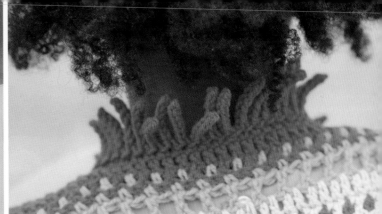

EDGING

Rnd 1: With RS facing, join A with a sc in first st to the left of right side seam on bottom edge of vest (**Note:** *For left-handed stitchers, begin at left side seam)*, sc in each st and sp across to next corner, 3 sc in corner st, PM in middle sc of 3-sc corner, working up right front, sc evenly up right front edge, working 1 sc in each row-end sc, and 2 sc in each row-end dc, sc in each ch across back neck, working down left front, sc evenly down left front edge, working 1 sc in each row-end sc, and 2 sc in each row-end dc, 3 sc in first st of hem, PM in middle sc of 3-sc corner, working across bottom edge, sc in each st and sp across, join with a sl st in first sc.

Work now progresses in a row.

Row 2: Sl st in each st to first marker, sl st in marked st, *ch 7, sl st in 2nd ch from hook and in next 5 ch, sl st in next sc; rep from * up right front edge, across back of neck, down left front to next marked st, sl st in each st across to next side seam. Fasten off, leaving rem sts unworked.

ARMHOLE EDGING

Rnd 1: With RS facing, join A with a sc at under-arm seam, sc evenly around, working 1 sc in each row-end sc, and 2 sc in each row-end dc around, join with a sl st in first sc.

Rep Armhole Edging around other armhole.

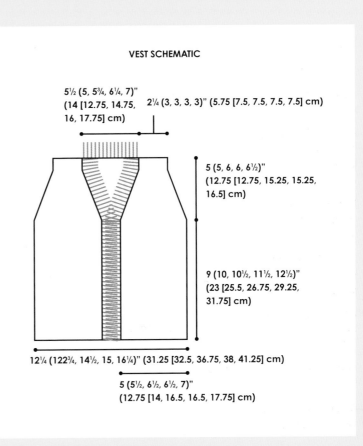

VEST SCHEMATIC

5½ (5, 5¾, 6¼, 7)" (14 [12.75, 14.75, 16, 17.75] cm)

2¼ (3, 3, 3, 3)" (5.75 [7.5, 7.5, 7.5, 7.5] cm)

5 (5, 6, 6, 6½)" (12.75 [12.75, 15.25, 15.25, 16.5] cm)

9 (10, 10½, 11½, 12½)" (23 [25.5, 26.75, 29.25, 31.75] cm)

12¼ (122¾, 14½, 15, 16¼)" (31.25 [32.5, 36.75, 38, 41.25] cm)

5 (5½, 6½, 6½, 7)" (12.75 [14, 16.5, 16.5, 17.75] cm)

chapter 3

Cozy
and Cool

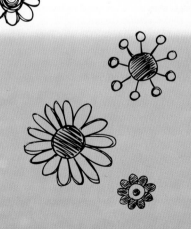

Windy City Scarf

An exciting array of colors and stripes make this scarf as fun to crochet as it is to wear. Crocheting between the stitches creates a bold texture that fits the bill for a boy's scarf. This scarf is perfect with a simple sweater or coat and a great pair of jeans. The Superwash Wool is so soft you will forget it is wool, and it comes in an amazing selection of colors!

Skill Level
Easy

Finished Size
4½" (11.5 cm) wide x 44" (112 cm) long, excluding fringe

Gauge
15 sts x 14 rows in hdc = 4" (10 cm). Take time to check gauge.

Yarn

Cascade 220 Superwash, 100% Superwash Wool, 3.5 oz (100 g)/220 yds (200 m) per skein: 1 skein each #811 Como Blue (A), #816 Gray (B), #1985 Duck Egg Blue (C), #817 Aran (D), #821 Daffodil (E), and #823 Burnt Orange (F)

Tools
I/9 (5.5 mm) crochet hook
J/10 (6 mm) crochet hook
yarn needle
rust-proof pins

Special Stitches Used

- *short single crochet (Ssc)*
  Insert hook in the horizontal lp below back lp of next st (on backside of work), yo, draw yarn through st, yo, draw through 2 lps on the hook.

SCARF

With smaller hook and A, ch 17.

Row 1: Working in back bump of ch sts, hdc in 3rd ch from hook, hdc in each ch across, turn—16 hdc.

Row 2: Ch 2 (counts as hdc here and throughout), hdc between first 2 sts, *hdc between next 2 sts; rep from * across, turn.

Rows 3–153: Rep Row 2 in the following color sequence: First Section: [18 more rows A, 3 rows B, 20 rows C]; Second Section: [3 rows A, 1 row D, 2 rows E, 1 row D, 3 rows A, 1 row D, 2 rows B, 1 row D, 3 rows A, 1 row D, 2 rows F, 1 row D, 3 rows A, 1 row D, 2 rows E, 1 row D, 3 rows A, 1 row D, 2 rows B, 1 row D, 3 rows A], Third Section: [21 rows F, 3 rows B, 20 rows E, 3 rows B, 20 rows A]. Fasten off at end of last row.

BOTTOM TRIM ROW

With WS of scarf facing, using larger hook, working across opposite side of foundation ch, join A with a sl st in first ch, ch 1, sc in each ch across. Fasten off.

EDGINGS

Note: *Edgings will be worked across sides of Sections 1 and 3 and ends of scarf, but not across Section 2.*

First Edging Row

With RS facing, and larger hook, join A with a sl st in first row-end st in first row of Section 2, ch 2, sk next row, *sl st in next row-end st, ch 1, sk next row*; rep from * to * across to corner, sl st in last row-end st at corner, turn to work across the bottom of the scarf, ssc in each sc across bottom edge of scarf, ch 1, turn to work up the other side of scarf, sl st in first row-end st, ch 1, sk next row; rep from * to * across to end of Section 1, sk last row of Section 1, sl st in first row-end st of Section 2. Fasten off.

Second Edging Row

Work in the same manner on the opposite side of the scarf, beg in the st at the end of the row in Section 2, rep First Edging Row across side of Section 3, top edge of scarf and opposite side of Section 3, ending with sl st in first row-end st of Section 2. Fasten off.

FRINGE

There are 7 Fringes on each end of the scarf.
Cut 56 strands of B, 10" (25 cm) long. With RS
facing, using larger hook, fold one fringe group
of 4 strands in half, insert hook between second
and third sts in second row from the edge, draw
folded end of fringe through st far enough to
bring the 8 tail ends through the loop, hook the
tail ends and draw through the folded loop and
tighten it to make a neat Girth Hitch Knot, which
keeps the edge of the scarf flat. Rep these instructions in every other st in second row, until you
have made a total of 7 fringes. Rep on the other
end of the scarf.

FINISHING

Weave in ends. Pin scarf out straight on a blocking board and wet or steam block. Trim the ends
of the Fringe Tassels if needed, to make them all
the same length.

Section 1

Section 2

Section 3

Caravan Scarf

This fashionable wrap is fringed with fanciful crocheted coins. Wear it tied in the back, in the front, or at the hip. The Caravan Scarf is a great pattern to show off a beautiful variegated yarn, and Superwash Wool is an excellent choice for softness and drape. To make a cute bandito, simply crochet fewer rows.

Special Stitches Used

- **Invisible Fasten Off**
  Cut yarn leaving a 3" (7.5 cm) tail. Insert hook in blo of first st in rnd, yo, and draw yarn all the way through the loop on the hook, as if to fasten off in the usual way. Insert the hook in both lps of next st, yo with tail end and pull through st. Finally, insert hook in flo of last st in rnd, yo, draw yarn down through.

- **Lazy Daisy stitch**
  An embroidery stitch used to embellish the Large Coins.

Skill Level
Easy

Finished Size
45" (114.5 cm) wide x 19" (48.5 cm) long, blocked, excluding coin fringe

Gauge
6 sts and 10 rows in dc = 4" (10 cm)

Yarn

Classic Elite Liberty Wool Print Light, 100% washable wool, 200 yd (183 m)/1.75 oz (50 g) per skein: 2 skeins #6690 Ultra Violet Autumn (A)

Classic Elite MillaMia, 100% extra fine merino, 136 yd (124 m)/1.75 oz (50 g) per skein: 1 skein each #143 Fuchsia (B), and #104 Claret (C)

Tools
G/6 (4mm) crochet hook

yarn needle

rust-proof pins

SCARF

With A, make a Magic Ring (see page 15).

Row 1: Insert hook into ring, yo and draw up a lp, ch 4, (2 dc, ch 4, 2 dc, tr) in ring, turn. Pull on tail end of yarn to close ring—4 dc; 2 tr; 2 ch-4 sps.

Row 2: Ch 4 (counts as tr here and throughout), 2 tr in first st, dc in each of next 2 sts, (2 dc, ch 4, 2 dc) in next ch-4 sp, dc in each of next 2 sts, 2 tr in last st, turn—8 dc; 5 tr; 2 ch-4 sps.

Row 3: Ch 4, 2 tr in first st, dc in each of next 5 sts, (2 dc, ch 4, 2 dc) in next ch-4 sp, dc in each of next 6 sts, 2 tr in last st, turn—15 dc; 5 tr; 2 ch-4 sps.

Rows 4–31: Ch 4, 2 tr in first st, dc in each st to next ch-4 sp, (2 dc, ch 4, 2 dc) in next ch-4 sp, dc in each st across to last st, 2 tr in last st, turn—211 dc; 5 tr; 2 ch-4 sps at end of last row. Fasten off.

SMALL COINS

Make 26 with B

Make a Magic Ring. Insert hook into ring and draw up lp, ch 3, work 12 dc in ring. Pull on tail end of yarn to close ring. Invisible Fasten Off.

LARGE COINS

Make 3 in yarn B

Make a Magic Ring. Insert hook into ring and draw up lp, ch 4, work 17 tr in ring. Pull on tail end of yarn to close ring. Invisible Fasten Off.

With A and a yarn needle, embroider a 4-petal Lazy Daisy on each of the Large Coins. Weave in ends on Scarf and Coins.

EDGINGS

Rnd 1: With RS side facing, join C with a sl st in top right-hand corner of scarf, inserting hook under second st from edge, yo and draw up a lp, ch 4, *sc under 2nd st from edge of next row, ch 3*, rep from * to * across the top edge to last row (to the corner), (2 sc in corner, then insert hook in same st, then into center hole of the back side of one Large Coin, yo and draw up lp large enough to allow the Coin and corner of the scarf to just meet, ch 1, 2 sc) all in corner st. Working across side edge, ch 3, sk next 2 sts, insert hook bet last skipped st and next st, then into center hole of the back side of a Small Coin, yo and draw up lp large enough to allow the Coin and the edge of the scarf to just meet, ch 1 (coin inserted), **[ch 2, sk next 2 sts, sc bet last skipped and next st] 3 times, ch 2, sk next 2 sts, insert a Small Coin bet last skipped st and next st, rep from ** 11 times, ch 2, (2 sc, insert a Large Coin, 2 sc) in corner st, rep from * to * 13 times. Ch 2, (2 sc, insert a Large Coin, sc) in last corner. Invisible Fasten Off.

FINISHING

Weave in ends. Pin the Scarf on a blocking board, and wet or steam block.

Hook placement for top edging

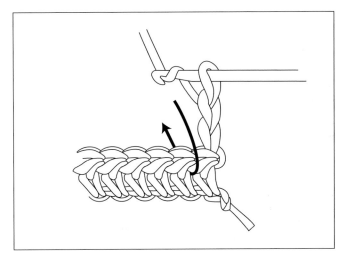

Inserting hook between stitches

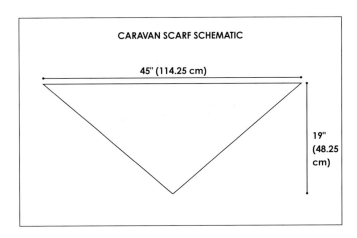

CARAVAN SCARF SCHEMATIC

45" (114.25 cm)

19" (48.25 cm)

Mohawk Earflap Hat

Boys will *ask* to wear this hat. Make it in his favorite colors and he'll still be wearing it when he arrives at his destination. Worked in basic stitches, this hat only looks difficult. It is made in a warm and durable cotton and wool blend, which easily weathers day-to-day wear all season long.

Skill Level
Easy

Finished Size
Directions are given for size S. Changes for M and L are in parentheses.
Circumference: 16 (18, 20)" (40.5 [45.5, 51] cm)

Gauge
First 3 rnds = 3¾" (9.5 cm); 14 sts = 4" (10 cm). Take time to check gauge.

Yarn

Spud & Chloë Sweater, 55% Superwash Wool, 45% cotton, 3.5 oz (100 g)/160 yd (146 m): 1 hank each #7504 Lake (A) and #7505 Firefly (B)

Tools
H/8 (5 mm) crochet hook
yarn needle

Notes: *All rounds are joined and turned. Hat rows are worked in the front or back loop only as indicated.*

HAT

With A, form an adjustable ring (see page 15).

Row 1 (RS): Ch 3 (counts as dc here and throughout), 9 dc in ring, tighten ring, join with a sl st in top beg ch-3, turn—10 dc.

Row 2 (WS): Ch 3, working in flo, dc in same st, 2 dc in each st around, join with a sl st in top beg ch-3, turn—20 dc.

Row 3: Ch 3, working in blo, dc in same st, 2 dc in each st around, join with a sl st in beg ch-3, turn—40 dc.

Row 4: Ch 3, working in flo, *dc in each of next 2 dc, 2 dc in next dc, rep from * around, join with sl st in top beg ch-3, turn—53 dc.

Size S Only

Row 5: Ch 3, working in blo, dc in each of next 11 sts, 2 dc in next st, *dc in each of next 9 sts, 2 dc in next st, rep from * around, join with a sl st in beg ch-3, turn—58 dc.

Sizes M and L Only

Row 5: Ch 3, working in blo, *dc in each of next 3 sts, 2 dc in next st, rep from * around, join with a sl st in beg ch-3, turn—66 dc.

Size M Only

Row 6: Ch 3, working in flo, dc in each st around, join with sl st in top beg ch-3, turn—66 sc.

Size L Only

Row 6: Ch 3, working in flo, dc in each of next 3 dc, 2 dc in next st, *dc in each of next 4 dc, 2 dc in next st, rep from * around, join with sl st in top beg ch-3, turn—74 dc.

All Sizes

Row 5 (7, 7): Ch 3, working in blo, dc in each st around, join with sl st in top beg ch-3, turn—53 (66, 78) sc.

Row 6 (8, 8): Ch 3, working in flo, dc in each st around, join with sl st in top beg ch-3, turn.

Rows 7–10 (9–12, 9–12): Rep last 2 rows twice.

Sizes S and L Only

Row 11 (13): Rep Row 5 (7) once.

Do not fasten off, continue to left earflap.

All Sizes

First Earflap

Note: Beg of rnd is back of hat.

Row 1: With WS (RS, WS) facing, ch 3, PM in top of ch-3 just made, working in flo (blo, flo), dc in each of next 23 sts, turn, leaving rem sts unworked—24 dc.

Row 2: Ch 3, working in blo (flo, blo), dc2tog over next 2 sts, dc in next 5 sts, dc2tog over next 2 sts, dc in next st, turn, leaving remaining sts unworked—9 dc.

Row 3: Ch 3, working in flo (blo, flo), dc2tog over next 2 sts, dc in next 3 sts, dc2tog over next 2 sts, dc in last st, turn—7 dc.

Row 4: Ch 3, working in blo (flo, blo), dc in each st across, turn.

Row 5: Ch 1, working in both loops of sts, sc2tog over next 2 sts, sc in next st, ch 26, sl st in 2nd ch from hook and in each of next 24 ch, sk 1 st on flap, sc in next st, sc2tog over next 2 sts. Fasten off.

Second Earflap

Row 1: With WS (RS, WS) facing, join A with a sl st in marked ch-3 at beg of Row 1 of first Earflap, working in blo (flo, blo), dc in each of next 24 sts, turn, leaving remaining sts unworked—24 dc.

Row 2: Ch 3, working in flo (blo, flo), dc2tog over next 2 sts, dc in next 5 sts, dc2tog over next 2 sts, dc in next st, turn, leaving remaining sts unworked—9 dc.

Row 3: Ch 3, working in blo (flo, blo), dc2tog over next 2 sts, dc in next 3 sts, dc2tog over next 2 sts, dc in last st, turn—7 dc.

Row 4: Ch 3, working in flo (blo, flo), dc in each st across, turn.

Row 5: Ch 1, working in both loops of sts, sc2tog over next 2 sts, sc in next st, ch 26, sl st in 2nd ch from hook and in each of next 24 ch, sk 1 st on flap, sc in next st, sc2tog over next 2 sts. Fasten off.

MOHAWK

Row 1: With RS facing, join B with dc around the post of the turning ch-3 of the last row of the Hat, 2 dc around same post, working toward center of hat, work 3 dc around the post of each ch-3 turning ch of each row to the crown, leaving equal number of sts on each side of hat, work 3 dc around the post of corresponding dc of Row 1 and each row to last row of Hat, turn—66 (72, 78) dc.

Row 2: *Ch 7, sl st in 2nd ch from hook and in next 5 ch, sk next dc, sl st in flo of next st, rep from * across, turn.

Row 3: Working in rem unused loops of Row 1, *ch 7, sl st in 2nd ch from hook and in next 5 ch, sk next dc, sl st in rem flo of next st, rep from * across. Fasten off B.

EDGING

With RS facing, join B with a sc at back of hat where the rows fastened off, ch 1, sc in each st to flap, *sc in each of next 5 row-end sts, 3 sc in corner of flap, sc in next 2 sts, sl st in each of next 25 tie sts, turn at end of Tie, sl st in each sl st across Tie to Flap, sc in next st, 2 sc in last st of Row 5 of flap*, sc in each dc to next earflap; rep from * to * once, sc in each st around to beg, join with sl st in first sc. Fasten off.

Weave in ends.

Rochelle Hat

In this fun hat, the clusters increase by one stitch in each round, creating more and more texture. The bottom band mimics ruched fabric, with long single crochet stitches serving as a complementary embellishment. For a splash of color, a scarf can be woven through the spaces in the last 2 rounds of clusters and tied in a knot on the side.

Special Stitches Used

- **2-dc cluster**
  [Yo, insert hook in st or sp, yo, draw up a lp, yo, draw yarn through 2 lps on hook] twice, yo and pull through 3 lps on hook.

- **3-dc cluster**
  [Yo, insert hook in st or sp, yo, draw up a lp, yo, draw yarn through 2 lps on hook] 3 times, yo and pull through 4 lps on hook.

- **4-dc cluster**
  [Yo, insert hook in st or sp, yo, draw up a lp, yo, draw yarn through 2 lps on hook] 4 times, yo and pull through 5 lps on hook.

- **5-dc cluster**
  [Yo, insert hook in st or sp, yo, draw up a lp, yo, draw yarn through 2 lps on hook] 5 times, yo and pull through 6 lps on hook.

- **6-dc cluster**
  [Yo, insert hook in st or sp, yo, draw up a lp, yo, draw yarn through 2 lps on hook] 6 times, yo and pull through 7 lps on hook.

- **7-dc cluster**
  [Yo, insert hook in st or sp, yo, draw up a lp, yo, draw yarn through 2 lps on hook] 7 times, yo and pull through 8 lps on hook.

- **8-dc cluster**
  [Yo, insert hook in st or sp, yo, draw up a lp, yo, draw yarn through 2 lps on hook] 8 times, yo and pull through 9 lps on hook.

- **9-dc cluster**
  [Yo, insert hook in st or sp, yo, draw up a lp, yo, draw yarn through 2 lps on hook] 9 times, yo and pull through 10 lps on hook.

- **10-dc cluster**
  [Yo, insert hook in st or sp, yo, draw up a lp, yo, draw yarn through 2 lps on hook] 10 times, yo and pull through 11 lps on hook.

- **11-dc cluster**
  [Yo, insert hook in st or sp, yo, draw up a lp, yo, draw yarn through 2 lps on hook] 11 times, yo and pull through 12 lps on hook.

Skill Level
Intermediate

Finished Size
Circumference:
19½" (49.5 cm)

From top of crown to brim: 6½" (16.5 cm)

Gauge
First 2 rnds = 2" (5 cm) in diameter; 5 sts = 1" (2.5 cm) on the brim of hat

Yarn

Universal Yarn Uptown DK, 100% acrylic, 273 yd (250 m)/3.5 oz (100 g): 1 skein #106 Bittersweet

Sizing
To fit a 20–21" (51–53.5 cm) head

Tools
G/6 (4 mm) crochet hook

yarn needle

scarf (optional): 38" (96.5 cm) long on the top edge, 43" (109 cm) long on the bottom edge, and 3" (7.5 cm) wide

Special Stitches Used *(cont.)*

- **Invisible Fasten Off (see page 14)**
  Cut yarn leaving a 3" (7.5 cm) tail. Insert hook in blo of first st in rnd, yo, and draw yarn all the way through the loop on the hook, as if to fasten off in the usual way. Insert the hook in both lps of next st, yo with tail end and pull through st. Finally, insert hook in flo of last st in rnd, yo, draw yarn down through.

- **long sc**
  Insert hook in designated st 7 rows below, yo, draw yarn through st, yo, draw yarn through 2 lps on hook.

HAT

Make a Magic Ring (see page 15).

Rnd 1 (WS): Insert hook into ring, yo, pull up a loop, work 15 dc into ring, join with a sl st in 2nd dc at beg of rnd. Pull on tail end of yarn to close ring—15 dc.

Rnd 2: Draw up a ½" (1.3 cm) lp, (2-dc cluster, ch 2) in each dc around, join with a sl st in first cluster—14 clusters.

Rnd 3: Draw up a ½" (1.3 cm) lp, (3-dc cluster, ch 3) in each ch-2 lp around, join with a sl st in first cluster.

Rnd 4: Draw up a ½" (1.3 cm) lp, (4-dc cluster, ch 4) in each ch-3 lp around, join with a sl st in first cluster.

Rnd 5: Draw up a ½" (1.3 cm) lp, (5-dc cluster, ch 4) in each ch-4 lp around, join with a sl st in first cluster.

Rnd 6: Draw up a ½" (1.3 cm) lp, (6-dc cluster, ch 4) in each ch-5 lp around, join with a sl st in first cluster.

Rnd 7: Draw up a ½" (1.3 cm) lp, (7-dc cluster, ch 4) in each ch-6 lp around, join with a sl st in first cluster.

Rnd 8: Draw up a ½" (1.3 cm) lp, (8-dc cluster, ch 4) in each ch-7 lp around, join with a sl st in first cluster.

Rnd 9: Draw up a ½" (1.3 cm) lp, (9-dc cluster, ch 4) in each ch-7 lp around, join with a sl st in first cluster.

Rnd 10: Draw up a ½" (1.3 cm) lp, (10-dc cluster, ch 4) in each ch-7 lp around, join with a sl st in first cluster.

Rnd 11: Draw up a ½" (1.3 cm) lp, (11-dc cluster, ch 4) in each ch-7 lp around, join with a sl st in first cluster.

Rnd 12: *Sc in blo of each of next 7 ch sts, sl st in both lps of next cluster, rep from * to around.

Rnd 13: *Ch 7, sk nxt 7 sc, sl st in next sl st, rep from * around.

Rnd 14: *Sc in blo of each of next 7 ch sts, sl st in next sl st, rep from * around.

Rnds 15–17: Rep Rnds 13–14 once, then rep Rnd 13 once.

Rnd 18: *Hdc in blo of next 7 ch sts, sl st in next sl st, 2 long sc in top of corresponding cluster in Rnd 11, rep from * to * around. Invisible Fasten Off.

FINISHING

The side that was facing you when you were crocheting the hat, is the wrong side. Turn the hat inside out to have the right side facing you. Weave in ends. A scarf can be woven into the spaces in Rnds 10 and 11, by alternating the *weaving in a space in Rnd 10, then in a space in Rnd 11, rep from * around. Tie the ends of the scarf in a square knot.

Hopscotch Leg Warmers

Step out and keep warm in style. These leg warmers can be worn inside boots to show off just the cuffs, or worn with shoes to let them take center stage. This wool blend yarn is warm and soft, and has a marvelous sheen and texture to make glorious pompoms. You may find that you want to make some of these eye-catching multicolored pom-poms to add to garments, scarves, and hats as well!

Special Stitches Used

- **foundation single crochet (fsc) (page 15)**
Start with a slip knot on hook, ch 2, insert hook in 2nd ch from hook, draw up a lp, yo, draw through 1 lp (ch made), yo, and draw through 2 lps—1 single crochet with its own chain at bottom. Work next stitch under lps of that chain. Insert hook under 2 lps at bottom of the previous stitch, draw up a lp, yo and draw through 1 lp, yo and draw through 2 lps. Repeat for length of foundation.

Skill Level
Easy

Finished Size
Directions are given for girl's size 6. Changes for 8 and 10 are in parentheses.

Finished Measurements
10 (11, 12)" [25 (28, 30.5) cm] long, with cuff folded; 8 (8, 8 ½)" (20 [20, 22] cm) wide at the bottom, when laid flat and not stretched.

Gauge
21 sts and 22 rows = 4" (10 cm) in sc in blo pattern of leg

Yarn

[4]

Cascade Pacific, 60% acrylic, 40% Superwash Merino Wool, 213 yd (195 m)/3.5 oz (100 g): 2 skeins #53 Beet (A), and 1 skein each #66 Teal Heather (B), #84 Persimmon (C), and #51 Honeysuckle Pink (D).

Tools
F/5 (3.75mm) crochet hook
size 1 3/8" (35 mm) pom-pom maker
yarn needle
rust-proof pins

LEG WARMERS (MAKE 2)

With A, ch 65 (70, 75).

Row 1 (RS): Working in back bar of the ch sts, sc in 2nd ch from hook and on next 47 (52, 57) ch, hdc in rem 16 ch, turn.

Row 2 (RS): Ch 2, working in blo only, *hdc in first 7 sts, ch 2, sk next 2 sts, hdc in next 7 sts, sc in each st across, turn.

Row 3: Ch 2, working in blo only, sc in each of first 48 (53, 58) sts, hdc in each sts across, turn.

Rows 4–49 (51, 53): Rep Rows 2–3 (23 [24, 25]) times. Fasten off, leaving a 20 (22, 24)" (51 [56, 61] cm) sewing length.

CUFF TRIM

With RS facing, join B with a sl st in top right-hand corner of the cuff (hdc end of Leg Warmer), *ch 4, sk next 2 rows, insert hook in the st that is 3 sts below the edge, right under the unworked front lp of the st, complete a long sc, rep from * across the top edge of the Cuff. Fasten off.

BOTTOM TRIM

With WS facing, with B, place slip knot on hook, yo, insert hook in the top right-hand corner (the last ch in the beg ch of the Leg Warmers), yo, draw yarn through st, [yo, draw yarn through 2 lps on hook] twice to complete a standing dc, dc in the edge st at the beg of row 1 of the Leg Warmers, *sk next row, dc in next row-end st, rep from * across bottom edge. Fasten off.

CUFF TIE (MAKE 2)

With B, work 163 (165, 167) fsc. Fasten off.

POM-POMS (MAKE 4)

On one half of the pom-pom maker, wrap yarn A
86 times. On the other half, wrap yarn A 5 times in
the middle, wrap yarn C 10 times on top of color
A, wrap yarn D 18 times on top of color C, wrap
yarn B 8 times on the right-hand side of color D,
and wrap yarn A 45 times on top of all previous
colors. Finish Pom-Pom as directed in pom-pom
maker instructions.

FINISHING

Weave in ends, except the long tails left for seam-
ing. Pin Leg Warmers and Cuff Ties on a blocking
board, and wet or steam block. Sew side seams
on the Leg Warmers from bottom edge up to
where the cuff folds (where the hdc sts begin).
Weave a Cuff Tie through the spaces in each of
the Cuffs, and tie a knot at the very end of each
Cuff Tie. Sew one Pom-Pom on each knotted end
of both Cuff Ties.

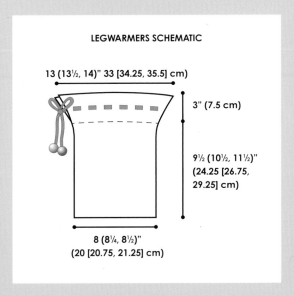

LEGWARMERS SCHEMATIC

13 (13½, 14)" 33 [34.25, 35.5] cm)

3" (7.5 cm)

9½ (10½, 11½)"
(24.25 [26.75,
29.25] cm)

8 (8¼, 8½)"
(20 [20.75, 21.25] cm)

His and Hers Mittens

Here are two pairs of mittens and two different styles of construction. Give them both a try! Change the colors and either pair could look great for a boy or a girl. The boy's mittens have classic boy striping so you can make them in his favorite colors. Worked from wrist to fingertip with a stretchy wrist band, they are great under a coat with the cuff up for added coverage. The girl's mittens have nubby texture and fingertip to wrist construction. Worked from the fingertip down to the cuff, these easy mittens are as unique and special as the hands they keep warm.

Special Stitches Used

- **5-dc cluster (Cl)**
  *Yo insert hook in indicated st, yo and draw up a loop, yo, draw through 2 loops on hook; rep from * 4 times in same st, yo, draw through all 6 loops on hook.

- **single crochet 2 together (sc2tog)**
  [Insert hook in next st, yo, draw yarn through st] twice, yo, draw yarn through 3 loops on hook.

Skill Level
Intermediate

Finished Size
Directions are given for children ages 3–6.

Gauge
14 sts and 11 rows hdc = 4" (10 cm). Take time to check gauge.

Yarn

3

Patons Classic Wool DK Superwash, 100% wool, 125 yd (114 m)/1.75 oz (50 g) per ball:1 ball each #12420 Pink (A), #12014 Latte (B) #12134 Royal Blue (C), #12011 Flagstone (D), and #12013 Mocha (E)

Tools
J/10 (6 mm) crochet hook

yarn needle

stitch marker

Notes: All rounds are joined then turned, unless otherwise stated. Place a st marker in first st of each Rnd and move as work progresses. Work over the unused strands of yarn and pick up colors when needed. Polka Dot Mittens are worked from fingertips to cuff. Striped Mittens are worked from cuff to fingertips.

POLKA DOT MITTENS (MAKE 2)

With A, ch 2.

Rnd 1 (RS): 6 sc in 2nd ch from hook, join with a sl st in first sc, turn—6 sc.

Rnd 2: Ch 1, 2 sc in next 2 sts, sc in next sc, 2 sc in next 2 sts, sc in next sc, join with sl st in first sc, turn—10 sc.

Rnd 3: Ch 1, sc in next sc, 2 sc in next 2 sts, sc in next 3 sc, 2 sc in next 2 sts, sc in next 2 sts, join with a sl st in first sc, turn—14 sc.

Rnd 4: Ch 1, sc in next 2 sc, 2 sc in next 2 sts, sc in each of next 5 sc, 2 sc in next 2 sts, sc in each of next 3 sc, join with sl st in first sc, turn—18 sc.

Rnd 5 (RS): Ch 1, *sc in each of next 3 sts, changing to B in last st, Cl in next st, changing color to A to complete the st, with A, sc in each of next 2 sts; rep from * twice, join with a sl st in first sc, turn—3 Cl in next st, 15 sc.

Rnd 6: Ch 1, sc in each st around, join with a sl st in first sc, turn—18 sc.

Rnd 7: Ch 1, sc in first sc, changing to B; *Cl in next st, changing to A to complete st**, with A, sc in next 5 sts; rep from * around, ending last rep at **, with A, sc in each of last 4 sc, join with a sl st in first sc, turn—3 Cl, 15 sc.

Rnd 8: Ch 1, *2 sc in next sc, sc in next 5 sts; rep from * around, join with a sl st in first sc, turn—21 sc.

Rnd 9: Ch 1, *sc in each of next 5 sts, changing to B to complete last st, Cl in next st, changing to A to complete st, sc in next st; rep from * around, join with a sl st in first sc, turn—3 Cl, 18 sc.

Rnd 10: With A, ch 1, *2 sc in next st, sc in each of next 6 sts; rep from * around, join with a sl st in first sc, turn—24 sc.

Rnd 11: Ch 1, *sc in each of next 2 sts, changing to B in last st, Cl in next st, changing to A to complete st, sc in each of next 5 sts; rep from * around, join with a sl st in first sc, turn—3 Cl, 21 sc.

Rnd 12: Ch 1, 2 sc in next sc, sc in next 7 sc; rep from * twice, join with a sl st in first sc, turn—27 sc.

Rnd 13: Ch 1, *with A, sc in next 8 sc, changing to B in last st, Cl in next st, changing to A to complete st; rep from * twice, join with sl st in first sc, turn—3 Cl in next st, 24 sc. (***Note:*** *If you keep working evenly for about 10 rnds, these would fit an adult.*) Proceed to Rnd 14.

Work now progresses in rows for Thumb Opening.

Row 14: Ch 1, sc in each of next 27 sts, turn—27 sts.

Row 15: Ch 1, *sc in each of next 4 sts, changing to B to complete last st, Cl in next st, changing to A to complete st, sc in next 4 sts; rep from * twice, turn.

Row 16: Ch 1, *sc in each of next 7 sts, sc2tog over next 2 sts; rep from * twice, turn—24 sc.

Work now progresses in joined rnds.

Rnd 17: Ch 1, *sc in each of next 6 sts, sc2tog over next 2 sts; rep from * twice, changing to B to complete last st, ch 1, JOIN with a sl st in first sc, turn—21 sc, 1 ch-1 sp.

Rnd 18: Ch 1, with B, 2 sc in next ch-1 sp, sc in each sc around, join with a sl st in first sc, turn—23 sc.

Rnd 19: Pick up A, with A, ch 1, sl st in each st around, join with sl st in first st, turn—23 sc.

Rnd 20: Ch 1, working over sts in Rnd 19, sc in each sc in Rnd 18, join with a sl st in first sc. DO NOT TURN.

Rnds 21–24: Ch 1, sc in each sc around, join with a sl st in first sc. DO NOT TURN.

Rnd 25: Pick up B, with B, ch 1, sl st in each st around, join with a sl st in first st. Fasten off.

With RS facing, make a slip knot with B, insert hook in any st between Rnds 21 and 22 and draw up a lp of B, with yarn strand in back of work, sl st in each st around. Fasten off.

Thumb

Ch 3, join with sl st in first ch to form a ring.

Rnd 1: Ch 1, 6 sc in ring, do not join. Work in a spiral, PM in first st of Rnd and move marker up as work progresses—6 sc.

Rnd 2: Sc in each sc around.

Rnd 3: 2 sc in each of next 2 sc, sc in last 4 sc—8 sc.

Rnds 4–5: Sc in each st around.

Work now progresses in rows.

Row 6: Sc in each of next 6 sts, turn, leaving remaining 2 sts unworked—6 sc.

Rows 7–8: Ch 1, sc in each st across, turn.

Row 9: Ch 1, sc2tog over next 2 sts, sc in next 2 sts, sc2tog over next 2 sts, turn—4 sts.

Row 10: Ch 1, [sc2tog over next 2 sts] twice—2 sts. Fasten off, leaving a long sewing length.

Finishing

With yarn needle and sewing length, sew Thumb into Thumb Opening.

STRIPED MITTENS (MAKE 2)

Cuff

With C, ch 17.

Row 1: Sc in 2nd ch from hook and in each ch across, turn—16 sc.

Rows 2–21: Ch 1, working in blo of sts, sc in each sc across, turn. At end of last row, fasten off leaving a 12" (30.5 cm) sewing length.

With yarn needle and sewing length, sew top of Row 21 to base of Row 1 to form a tube.

Wrist Edging

Rnd 1: Join C with a sl st in any row-end st on one side of Cuff, sc in each row-end st around, join with a sl st in first sc—(21 sc). Fasten off.

Mitten Body

Note: *All rnds are worked with RS facing. Do not turn at ends of rnds.*

Rep Wrist Edging Rnd 1 on opposite side of cuff. Do not fasten off.

Rnd 2: Ch 1 (does not count as a st here and throughout), hdc in same st and in each st around, join with a sl st in top of first hdc (skipping the first ch that is not a st)—21 hdc. Drop C, pick up D.

Rnd 3: With D, ch 1, hdc in same st, hdc in each of next 5 hdc, *2 hdc in next hdc, hdc in each of next 6 hdc; rep from * once, 2 hdc in last st; join with a sl st in first hdc—24 hdc. Drop D, pick up E.

Rnd 4: With E, ch 1, hdc in same st, hdc in each of next 6 hdc, *2 hdc in next st, hdc in each of next 7 hdc; rep from * once, 2 hdc in last st; join with a sl st in first hdc—27 hdc. Drop E, pick up D.

Rnd 5: With D, ch 1, sc in each st around; join with a sl st in first sc—27 sc. Drop D, pick up C.

Rnd 6: With C, ch 1, hdc in first st, hdc in each of next 10 sts, sk next 8 sts for Thumb Opening, hdc in each of last 8 sts, join with a sl st in first hdc—19 hdc. Drop C, pick up D.

Rnds 7–9: With D, Ch 1, hdc in each st around, join with a sl st in first sc—19 sc. Drop D, pick up E.

Rnd 10: With E, ch 1, sc in each st around, join with a sl st in first sc—19 sc. Drop E, pick up C.

Rnd 11: With C, ch 1, sc in each st around, join with a sl st in first sc.

Rnd 12: With C, ch 1, sc in each of first 4 sts, *sc2tog over next 2 sts, sc in each of next 3 sts; rep from * around, join with a sl st in first sc—16 sc.

Rnd 13: Ch 1, sc in each st around, join with a sl st in first sc.

Rnd 14: Ch 1, sc in first 2 sc, *sc2tog over next 2 sts, sc in each of next 2 sts; rep from * 3 times, sc2tog over last 2 sts, join with a sl st in first sc—12 sc.

Rnd 15: Ch 1, sc in each st around, join with a sl st in first sc.

Rnd 16: Ch 1, [sc2tog over next 2 sts] 6 times, join with a sl st in first sc—6 sc.

Fasten off, leaving an 8" (20.5 cm) sewing length.

Turn mitten inside out. With yarn needle and sewing length, sew Rnd 10 closed. Weave in end. Turn mitten right side out.

Thumb

Rnd 1: With RS facing, join C with a sl st in first skipped st at base of Thumb Opening, ch 1, hdc in same st, hdc in each of next 8 skipped sts, hdc in next st (already used), sc through 2 mitten body sts at the same time, do not join. Work in a spiral, place marker in first st of Rnd and move marker up as work progresses—10 hdc, 1 sc.

Rnd 2: Sc in each st around—11 sc.

Rnd 3: [Sc in next st, sc2tog over next 2 sts] 3 times, sc in each of last 2 sts—8 sc.

Rnd 4: Sc in each st around.

Rnd 5: [Sc2tog over next 2 sts] 4 times—4 sc. Fasten off, leaving a 6" (15 cm) sewing length. With yarn needle and sewing length, sew together remaining four stitches to close thumb.

Finishing

Flip up cuff. Join E with sc in any st, sc in each st around; join with a sl st in first sc. Fasten off.

Skip to My Lou Slippers

A girl's slippers can be just as stylish as her best party shoes. A mix of colors paired with a unique bow embellishment make this pair eye-catching and fun. The slippers are easy to customize, since the toe is crocheted first. You can try them on her as you work to make them the perfect length. For a simpler version, omit the bow to show off the stripes.

Special Stitches Used

- *2 double crochet cluster (Cl)*
  [Yo, insert hook into indicated st, yo and draw up a lp, yo and pull through 2 sts] twice in same st, yo and draw through 3 lps on hook.

- *front post half double crochet (FPhdc)*
  Yo, insert hook from front to back to front again around the post of next st, yo and draw up a loop, yo and draw through 3 loops on hook.

- *Invisible Fasten Off (page 14)*
  Cut yarn leaving a 3" (8 cm) tail. Insert the hook into the blo of the first st of the rnd, yo, and pull the yarn all the way through the lp on hook, as if to fasten off in the usual way. Insert hook in both lps of next st, yo with tail end and pull through st. Finally, insert the hook in the front lp only of last st in rnd, yo, pull yarn down through.

Skill Level
Intermediate

Finished Measurements
Directions are given for children ages 3–6.

Gauge
Length: 7 (8, 9)" (18 [20.5, 23] cm)

Size: Directions are given for size Small (12–1). Changes for Medium (2–3) and Large (4–5) are in parentheses.

Gauge: 24 sts = 4" (10 cm). Take time to check gauge.

Yarn

Cascade Yarns Cherub DK, 55% nylon, 45% acrylic, 180 yd (165 m)/1.75 oz (50 g): 1 skein each #25 red (A), #19 orange (B) and #14 peach (C)

Tools
D/3 (3.25 mm) crochet hook
E/4 (3.50 mm) crochet hook
yarn needle
rust-proof pins
two ¾" (2 cm) D-rings

SLIPPER (MAKE 2)

Toe

With A, and E/4 hook, form an adjustable ring (page 15).

Rnd 1: Ch 3 (counts as dc here and throughout), work 8 (9, 10) dc in ring, join with a sl st in top of beg ch-3. Tighten ring.

Rnd 2: Ch 3, dc in first st (counts as first cluster), Cl in same st, 2 CL in each dc around, join with a sl st in top of beg ch-3—18 (20, 22) sts.

Rnd 3: Ch 2 (counts as hdc here and throughout), hdc in first st, hdc in next st, *2 hdc in next st, hdc in next st; rep from * around, join with sl st in top of beg ch-2— 27 (30, 33) hdc.

Rnds 4–12 (13, 14): Ch 2, FPhdc around the post of each st around, join with sl st in top of beg ch-2. Drop A to wrong side to be picked up later.

Sole

Row 1: With right side facing, join B with a sl st in first s, ch 1, sc in each st around, join with a sl st in first sc, turn. Drop B to wrong side to be picked up later.

Row 2: With right side facing, join C with a sl st in first st, ch 1, 2 sc in first st, sc each st across to last 2 sts, 2 sc in next st, sc in last st, turn—29 (32, 35) sc. Drop C to wrong side to be picked up later; pick up A.

Row 3: With A, ch 1, sc in first 3 sts, hdc in each st across to last 3 sts, sc in last 3 sts, turn.

Row 4: Ch 1, sc in each st across, turn. Drop A, pick up B.

Row 5: With B, rep Row 4. Drop B, pick up C.

Row 6: With C, rep Row 4. Drop C, pick up A.

Rows 7–28 (32, 36): Rep Rows 3–6 (5 [6, 7]) times; then rep Rows 3–4 once.

Trim

With B and D/3 hook, ch 3.

Row 1: (Sc, ch 2, sc) in 3rd ch from hook, turn.

Row 2: Ch 2, (sc, ch 2, sc) in next ch-2 sp.

Rows 3–49 (55, 61): Rep Row 2.

Buckle Bow

With A and E/4 hook, ch 18.

Row 1: Working in the back bump of ch sts, sc in 2nd ch from hook and in each ch across, turn—17 sc.

Rows 2–5: Ch 1, sk first st (dec made), sc in each st to last 2 sts, sk next st, sc in last st (dec made), turn—9 sc at end of last row.

Rows 6–10: Ch 1, 2 sc in first st, sc in each st to last st. 2 sc in last st, turn. Fasten off A.

Buckle Bow Edging

With right side facing, join C in last st ch 1, 2 sc in same st, working across left side of forked edge, work 4 sc evenly spaced across to row 6, work 4 sc evenly spaced across to next corner, sc in each st across bottom edge of bow; rep from* once, work Invisible Fasten off.

Buckle

With D/3 (3.25mm) and B, ch 6.

Rnd 1: Working in the back bump of the ch sts, sl st in 2nd ch from hook, sl st in each ch across (Buckle Divider formed), remove loop from hook, pick up a D-ring and place it on top of the Buckle Divider. Beg in the middle of the flat side of the D-ring, insert hook into the ring, then, back into the working lp and ch 1 around the ring. Insert the hook back in top end of the Buckle Divider and sc around the ring, work 20 more sc around the ring, [insert hook in bottom end of Buckle Divider and sc around ring] twice, work 20 more sc around the ring, work Invisible Fasten off.

Assembly

Weave in ends. Pin slipper Soles and Buckle Bows on a blocking board and wet or steam block.

To make the heel seam, fold the slipper Sole in half with right sides together and use an E/4 hook to work through double thickness, join A with a sl st in first st at bottom of heel, sl st in each row-end st across joining heel seam. Fasten off A.

Trim

The Trim will be crocheted to the top edges of the Sole and Toe in the following manner: Begin at the heel seam, lay the Trim on top of the slipper at the top edge, working in the holes running down the middle of the Trim and one st in from the edges of the Sole and Toe, insert the hook into the hole at the end of the trim, and then into the heel seam, *yo and draw up a loop, [insert hook in next st in Trim and into stripe of A on Sole, yo and pull up a loop, then draw lp through lp already on hook (sl st made)] twice, insert hook in next st of Trim and in between stripes of A and B, yo, draw up a lp, and draw through lp (sl st made); rep from * 6 (7, 8) times across to Toe, working across sts of Toe, **insert hook in next st in Trim and in next st of Toe, yo and draw up a lp, draw lp on hook (sl st made); rep from ** across Toes sts, working down other side of sole: **insert hook in next st of Trim and in between stripes of A and B, yo, draw up a lp, and draw through lp (sl st made), [insert hook in next st in Trim and into stripe of A on Sole, yo and pull up a lp, then draw lp through lp already on hook (sl st made)] twice**, rep from ** to ** 6 (7, 8) times to heal seam, overlap the last hole in the Trim over the beg hole and insert hook into both holes, and then into heel seam, yo and draw up a lp through all layers, pull this lp through lp already on hook. Fasten off.

Finishing

Weave in ends. With right sides facing up, weave Buckle Ribbons into Buckles, covering the Buckle Divider. Flatten the slipper to find the center of the Toes, and sew the Buckle Dividers to the centers of the Toes. Turn the sts in the middle of the top of the Buckles inward and tack in place, to make them look like hearts.

chapter 4

On the Go

Ellie Backpack

Bright cotton yarn makes this backpack a magnet for little girls on the go. Roomy enough to hold the day's necessities, it even has a secret pocket in the flap that buttons closed to secure treasures.

Special Stitches Used

- *pattern stitch worked in rnds (patt)*
  Rnd 1: Ch 1 (does not count as a st), sc in each st around, join with a sl st in first sc.

  Rnd 2: Ch 1, sc in first st, *hdc in next st, dc in next 3 sts, hdc in next st**, sc in next 3 sts; rep from * around, ending last rep at **, sc in last 2 sts, join with a sl st in first sc.

  Rnd 3: Ch 1 (does not count as a st), sc in each st around, join with a sl st in first sc.

  Rnd 4: Ch 1 (does not count as a st), dc in first st, *hdc in next st, sc in next 3 sts, hdc in next st **, dc in next 3 sts; rep from * around, ending last rep at **, dc in last 2 sts, join with a sl st in first dc.

  Rep Rnds 1–4 for patt.

Skill Level
Intermediate

Finished Size
10" (25.5 cm) wide x 10½" (26.5 cm) deep

Gauge
16 sts = 4" (10 cm); 8 rows = 2½" (6.5 cm). Take time to check gauge.

Yarn

Lily Sugar 'n Cream, 100% cotton, 2.5 oz (70 g)/120 yd (109 m): 2 balls #95 Red (A), 1 ball each #1699 Tangerine (B) and #73 Sunshine (C)

Tools
G/6 (4 mm) crochet hook

five 1" (2.5 cm) steel rings

swivel clasp

yarn needle

stitch markers

three 1" (2.5 cm) buttons (Sample uses Loops & Threads buttons, item #141062, purchased at Michael's)

sewing needle and matching sewing thread

BASE

With A, ch 32.

Row 1 (RS): Working in the back bump of ch sts, sc in 2nd ch from hook and in each ch across, turn—31 sc.

Rows 2–7: Ch 1, sc in each st across, turn. Do not turn at end of last row.

BAG

Rnd 1 (RS): Ch 1, working across short edge, sc in each of next 7 row-end sts, working across opposite side of foundation ch, ch 1, working across bottom edge of Base, sc in each of next 15 ch, pm, sc in next 16 sts, ch 1, working across short edge, sc in each of next 7 row-end sts, ch 1, pm, working across top edge of Base, sc in next 31 sts, changing to B, join with a sl st in first ch-1 sp—80 sts, including 4 ch-1 corners. Drop A to be picked up later.

Notes: On next rnd, treat each ch-1 sp as a st, and move marker up as work progresses. Always carry one unused color with every round to add density to the bag—80 sts, 2 rings placed. Carry remaining unused color on wrong side to be picked up later.

Rnd 2 (ring row): With B, ch 1, sc in first st, *hdc in next st, dc in next 3 sts, hdc in next st**, sc in next 3 sts*; rep from * to * 5 times, holding one ring against right side of bag, working over ring, dc in next 3 sts, hdc in next st, sc in next 3 sts; rep from * to * twice, holding one ring against right side of bag, working over ring, dc in next 3 sts, hdc in next st, sc in next 3 sts; ending last rep at **, sc in last 2 sts, join with a sl st in first sc (Row 2 of Patt complete)—10 pattern reps; 2 Back bottom strap rings placed. Drop B, join C.

Rnds 3–12: Starting with Row 3 of Patt, work even in Patt in the following color sequence: *1 rnd C, 1 rnd A, 1 rnd B; rep from * throughout.

Rnd 13 (ring row): With A, Ch 1, sc in each st to one st before the marked stitch in the middle of the front long side, holding a ring against the RS of the fabric, working over the ring, sc in the marked st and next 2 sts, remove marker, sc in st around, join with sl st in first sc—Rnd 1 of Patt complete, ring for clasp placed on center Front. Fasten off A, pick up B.

Rnds 14–30: Starting with B and working Row 2 of Patt, work even in Patt for 17 rnds, ending with Rnd 4 of Patt, with C. Fasten off C.

Rnd 31: With A, lay bag flat with Back facing, place markers for 2 strap rings directly above bottom strap rings, ch 1, *sc in each st across to marker, working over ring, sc in next 3 sts; rep from * once, sc in each st around, join with sl st in first sc. **Note:** *Double check that rings are in desired position. Fasten off.*

TIP: If you use split rings instead of solid rings, you can remove them and move them to the right spot or add them after crocheting the backpack.

FLAP

Starting at bottom of Flap, with A, ch 33.

Rnd 1 (RS): Working in the back bump of ch sts, sc in 2nd ch from hook and in each ch across, working across opposite side of foundation ch, sc in each ch across, changing to B in last sc, join with sl st in first sc—64 sc.

Rnd 2 (clasp round): With B, ch 1, dc in first sc, hdc in next st, sc in next 3 sts, hdc in next st, dc in next 3 sts, hdc in next st, sc in next 3 sts, hdc in next st, place clasp against fabric, working over the ring part of the clasp, (dc in next 3 sts, hdc in next st), sc in next 3 sts, *hdc in next st, dc in next 3 sts, hdc in next st, sc in next 3 sts; rep from * 4 times, hdc in next st, dc in each of last 2 sts, changing to C in last st; join with sl st in top first dc, skipping the first ch-1.

Rnds 3–18: Starting with C and working Row 1 of Patt, work even in Patt in established color sequence, ending with Rnd 4 of Patt, with C.

Rnd 19 (buttonhole rnd): With A, ch 1, sc in each of next 42 sts, *ch 3, sk next 3 sts, sc in next 5 sts; rep from * twice, sc in each st around, join with sl st in first sc.

Rnd 20: Ch 1, sc in each st and ch around, join with sl st in first sc—64 sc.

Rnd 21: Ch 1, sc in each st around, join with sl st in first sc. Fasten off A.

ASSEMBLY

With needle and matching thread, sew buttons on the inside of Flap opposite buttonholes.

With right sides facing, center top of Flap (open end) between upper strap rings on back of the bag. With wrong side of Flap facing, join A with a sl st in first st on back side of Flap and first sc of back of Bag, working through double thickness, ch 1, sc in first 32 sts. Fasten off A.

STRAPS (MAKE AND JOIN 2)

Row 1: With A, ch 57, sc in 2nd ch from hook, *hdc in next ch, dc in each of next 3 ch, hdc in next ch**; sc in next 3 ch; rep from * across, ending last rep at **, sc in last 2 ch, changing to B in last st, turn. Fasten off A.

Row 2: With B, ch 1, sc in each st across, changing to C in last sc, turn. Fasten off B.

Row 3: With C, ch 3 (counts as first dc), *hdc in next st, dc in next 3 sts, hdc in next st**; sc in next 3 sts; rep from * across, ending last rep at **, sc in last 2 sts, changing to A in last st, turn.

Row 4: With A, ch 1, sc in each st across, do not turn.

Row 5: Hold the strap rows with short end of strap against a ring at the bag base, and working over ring, sc in each of next 4 row-end sts, sl st in next st, turn.

Row 6: Ch 1, skip sl st just made, sl st in each of the 4 sc, rotate to work along Row 4, ch 1 sc in first st, *hdc in next st, dc in next 3 sts, hdc in next st**; sc in next 3 sts; rep from * across, ending last repeat at **, sc in last 2 sts, do not turn.

Row 7: Rotate to work along 2nd short side, attaching to the strap ring at the top of the bag, ch 1, hold ring to back of fabric, working through ring, sc in each of next 4 row-end sts, turn.

Row 8: Ch 1, sl st in next 4 sc. Fasten off A.

Graphic Messenger Bag

A rugged cotton fabric with bold stripes makes this bag ready for any boy. Cool buckles keep the bag closed as he makes his way to the skate park or the tree house in the woods. The graphic styling makes a statement as he makes his way in the world.

Skill Level
Intermediate

Finished Size
Bag: 12½" (31.5 cm) wide x 10½" (26.5 cm) deep (with base tucked in).
Strap: 33" (84 cm) long

Gauge
16 sts and 16 rows in sc = 4" (10 cm).
Take time to check gauge.

Yarn

Lion Brand Cotton Ease, 50% cotton, 50% acrylic, 3.5 oz (100 g)/207 yd (188 m): 2 skeins #152 Charcoal (A); 1 skein each #134 Terracotta (B) and #149 Stone (C)

Tools
I/9 (5.5 mm) crochet hook

locking stitch markers

yarn needle

four ¾" (2 cm) Pepperell Crafts Parachute Cord ™ Buckles (item code PCBUCK20), available at: www.pepperell.com.

Notes: *Drop colors to the back when not in use, pick up the color to begin a round. Take care not to accidentally increase or decrease at the join.*

BAG BODY

Starting a left side of Front, with B, ch 31.

Row 1 (RS): Sc in 2nd ch from hook and in each ch across, turn—30 sc.

Rows 2–5: Ch 1, sc in each st across, switching to A in the last st of last row.

Rows 6–95: Work even in sc, working in the following color sequence: 2 rows A, 1 row C, 1 row A, 1 row B, 85 rows A. Do not fasten off.

Joining Row: Fold Body in half with right sides facing, and, matching sts in foundation ch and top of Row 95, ch 1, working through double thickness, sc in each st across. Do not fasten off. Turn tube right-side out.

Bottom Edging

Ch 1, sc in each row-end st around, join with a sl st in first sc. Fasten off. This round will connect to the base.

Bag Base

With B, ch 49.

Rnd 1 (RS): Sc in 2nd ch from hook and in each ch across, working across the opposite side of foundation ch, sc in each ch across, do not join—96 sc. Work in a spiral. Place marker in first st of rnd and move marker up as work progresses.

Rnds 2–4: Sc in each st around—96 sc. Change to A in last st of Rnd 4.

Rnd 5: With A, sc in each st around.

Choose one long side of Base to be the "front". Pin one clasp in place approximately 6 sts in from each end of front.

Rnd 6 (joining buckles): *Sc in each st around to next pinned buckles, working through the bottom half of the buckle, sc in next 3 sts; rep from * once, sc in each rem st around, do not join.
Note: *You may need to switch to a smaller hook (I used an E) for getting the stitches through the buckle.*

Rnd 7: With wrong sides facing, hold Base Rnd 6 next to Bottom Edging of Body, aligning left side of Base with left side seam of Body, working through double thickness, sl st in each st around, join with a sl st in first sl st. Fasten off.

Bag Body Top Edging

Row 1: With RS facing, join A with sc in side of any body row at the top of the bag, sc in each row-end st around, join with a sl st in first sc. Fasten off.

BAG FLAP

Work same as Bag Body through Row 43. Do not fasten off A.

Flap Edging

Rnd 1: With A, ch 1, working down long side of Flap, sc in each row-end st across to next corner, 3 sc in corner st, working across foundation ch, sc in each ch across to next corner, 3 sc in corner st, working across other long edge to next corner 3 sc in next corner st, sc in each row-end st across to next corner, 3 sc in corner st, working across top of Row 43, sc in each sc across, join with a sl st in first sc. Fasten off.

Rnd 2: Line up the top halves of the buckles and pin them in place along the bottom long flap edge to align with buckle bottoms, ch 1, *sc in each st across to next corner, 3 sc in corner sc*; rep from * to * once, **sc in each sc across to next buckle, working through buckle opening, sc in next 3 sts; rep from ** once, rep from * to * twice, join with a sl st in first sc. Fasten off.

ASSEMBLY

With right sides facing, holding the nonbuckle edge of the flap to the back of Bag Body, using yarn needle and A, matching sts, whipstitch Flap onto Bag Body.

STRAP

With A, ch 105

Row 1: Sc in 2nd ch from hook and in each ch across, turn—104 sc.

Rows 2–5: Ch 1, sc in each sc across. Do not fasten off.

Strap Edging

Working across short edge, sl st in each row-end st across, s; st in each st across long edge; rep from * once, join with a sl st in first sl st. Fasten off, leaving a 12" (30.5 cm) tail. With yarn needle and A, sew one end of Strap to each end of top edge of Bag Body.

Prim Wristers

These great wristers pack a little bit of warmth with a huge amount of style! Made with a wool/silk blend yarn, these mitts are warm and soft. She'll want a pair in every color, and, using less than one hank per pair, you'll be able to accommodate her.

Skill Level
Intermediate

Finished Size
5" (12.5 cm) long x 4" (10 cm) wide at widest point (steam blocked). To fit child, age 10.

Gauge
10 sts = 1¾" (4.5 cm); 10 FPdc rows = 2¾" (7 cm); 11 hdc rows = 4" (10 cm). Take time to check gauge.

Yarn

Spud & Chloë Fine, 80% Superwash Wool, 20% silk, 5 oz (65 g)/248 yd (227 m): 1 skein #7808 Sassafras

Tools
G/6 (4 mm) crochet hook

tapestry needle

Special Stitches Used

- *foundation dc (fdc)*
  Start with a slip knot, ch 3, yo, insert hook in 3rd ch from hook, draw up a lp, yo, draw through 1 lp, (yo, and draw through 2 lps) twice—1 double crochet with its own chain at bottom. Work next stitch under lps of that chain. Yo, insert hook under 2 lps at bottom of the previous stitch, draw up a lp, yo and draw through 1 lp, (yo and draw through 2 lps) twice. Repeat for length of foundation.

- *shell* (2 dc, ch 1, 2 dc) in same st or sp.

- *back post double crochet (BPdc)*
  Yo, insert hook from front to back to front again around the post of next st, yo, draw yarn through, [yo, draw yarn through 2 lps on hook] twice.

- *front post double crochet (FPdc)*
  Yo, insert hook from front to back to front again around the post of next st, yo, draw yarn through, [yo, draw yarn through 2 lps on hook] twice.

- *single crochet 2 together (sc2tog)*
  [Insert hook in next st, yo, draw yarn through st] twice, yo, draw yarn through 3 lps on hook.

CUFF (MAKE 2)

Row 1 (RS): Work 10 fdc, turn.

Row 2: Ch 2 (counts as dc here and throughout), FPdc in each st across to last st, dc in last st—2 dc; 8 FPdc.

Rows 3–20: Ch 2, turn, FPdc in each st across to last st, dc in last dc—2 dc; 8 FPdc.

Fasten off leaving an 8" (20.5 cm) sewing length. With yarn needle and sewing length, matching sts, sew Row 1 to Row 20 forming a tube.

FOREARM EDGING

With right side facing, join A with sc in seam, sc in first row-end st, 2 sc in each row-end st around, join with a sl st in first sc—40 sc. Fasten off.

HAND EDGING

With right side facing, join A with sc in seam on opposite side of cuff, sc in first row-end st, 2 sc in each row-end st around, join with a sl st in first sc—40 sc. Do not fasten off.

WRISTER BODY

Note: All rows are turned. Some rows are joined. Some rows are NOT joined in order to make a thumbhole.

Rnd 1: Ch 3 (counts as dc here and throughout), sk first 3 sts, shell in next st, sk next 2 sts, dc in next 3 sts, *dc in next st, sk next 2 sts, shell in next st, sk next 2 sts, dc in next 2 sts; rep from * around, join with sl st in top of beg ch-3, turn—5 shells.

Rnd 2 (inc rnd): Ch 3, BPdc around the post of next 2 sts, sk next dc of shell, BPdc around the post of next dc, shell in next ch-1 sp, BPdc around the post of next dc, sk next dc of shell, BPdc around the post of next 3 sts, *sk next dc, BPdc around the post of next dc, shell in next ch-1 sp, BPdc around the post of next dc, sk next dc**, BPdc around the post of next 3 sts; rep from * around, ending last rep at **, join with sl st in top beg ch-3, turn.

Work now progresses in rows.

Row 3: Ch 3, *sk next 2 dc, FPdc around the post of next dc, shell in next ch-1 sp, FPdc around the post of next dc, sk 2 sts**, FPdc around the post of next 3 dc; rep from * around, ending last rep at **, FPdc around the post of next 2 dc, DO NOT JOIN, turn.

Row 4: Ch 3, BPdc around the post of next st, *sk next 2 sts, BPdc around the post of next st, shell in next ch-1 sp, BPdc around the post of next st, sk next 2 sts**, BPdc around the post of next 3 sts; rep from * around, ending last repeat at **, dc in last st, DO NOT JOIN, turn.

Row 5: Ch 3, *sk next 2 sts, FPdc around the post of next st, shell in next ch-1 sp, FPdc in next st, sk next 2 sts**, FPdc around the post of next 3 sts; rep from * around; ending last rep at **, FPdc around the post of next st, dc in last st, DO NOT JOIN, turn.

Work now progresses in joined rnds.

Rnd 6: Ch 3, BPdc around the post of next st, *sk 2 sts, BPdc around the post of next st, shell in next ch-1 sp, BPdc around the post of next st, sk next 2 sts**, BPdc around the post of next 3 sts; rep from * around, ending last rep at **, dc in last st, join with sl st in top beg ch-3.

Rnd 7 (dec rnd): Ch 3 (does not count as a st), FPdc around the post of next st, *sk next 3 sts, shell in next ch-1 sp, sk next 3 sts**, FPdc around the post of next 3 sts; rep from * around, ending last rep at **, FPdc around the post of last 2 dc, sk the beg ch-3, join with sl st in fist FPdc, turn.

Rnd 8: Ch 3, BPdc around the post of next 2 sts, *sk next 2 sts, shell in next ch-1 sp, sk next 2 sts**, BPdc around the post of next 3 sts; rep from * around, ending last rep at **, BPdc in last st; join with sl st in top beg ch-3, turn.

Rnd 9: Ch 1, sc in first st, *sc in each of next 6 sts and ch sts, sc2tog over next 2 sts; rep from * around, join with sl st in first sc—36 sc. Fasten off.

Zebra Cropped Hoodie

Take a walk on the wild side with this zebra-inspired cropped hoodie. Cropped styling and graphic stripes are fun details, but it is the fun, loopy texture that will drive her wild. This repetitive stitch pattern is easy to memorize and will stitch up quickly!

Special Stitches Used

- **half double crochet 2 together (hdc2tog)**
  [Yo, insert hook in next st, yo, draw yarn through st] twice, yo, draw yarn through all lps on hook.

Skill Level
Intermediate

Finished Size
Directions are given for girl's size 4. Changes for 6, 8, 10, and 12 are in parentheses.

Finished Chest: 24¼ (29, 30, 31½, 34)" (61.5 [73.5, 76, 80, 86.5] cm)

Finished Length: 8¼ (9¼, 10¼, 11¼, 12¼)" (21 [23.5, 26, 28.5, 31] cm)

Gauge
12 sts and 16 rows in Back and Front pattern = 4" (10 cm); 14 sts and 11 rows hdc = 4" (10 cm) in Sleeves and Hood pattern. Take time to check gauge.

Yarn

Cascade 220 Superwash Sport, 100% Superwash Merino Wool, 1.75 oz (50 g)/136 yd (124 m): 2 (2, 3, 3, 4) hanks #871 White (A), 2 (3, 3, 4, 5) hanks #815 Black (B), and 2 (2, 3, 3, 4) hanks #807 Raspberry (C)

Tools
I/9 (5.5 mm) crochet hook

yarn needle

Notes: On Row 1, the first 2 skipped ch sts don't count as a st. Ch 1 at beginning of row or round does not count as a st unless otherwise stated.

COLOR SEQUENCE

Work Back and Fronts in the following color sequence: *2 rows A, 2 rows B, rep from * throughout.

BACK

With A, ch 42 (44, 46, 48, 52).

Row 1 (RS): Hdc in 3rd ch from hook and in each ch across, turn—40 (42, 44, 46, 50) hdc.

Row 2 (WS): Working in flo, ch 1, sc in first hdc, (ch 3, sc) in each hdc across, complete last sc with B, turn. Drop A to be picked up later.

Row 3: Ch 1, working in rem unused lps 2 rows below, hdc in each hdc across, turn.

Row 4: With B, working in flo, ch 1, sc in first hdc, (ch 3, sc) in each hdc across, pick up A from 2 rows below and complete last sc with A, turn. Drop B to be picked up later.

Row 5: With A, rep Row 3.

Row 6: With A, rep Row 4, pick up B from 2 rows below and complete last sc with B, turn. Drop A to be picked up later.

Rows 7–16 (18, 20, 22, 24): Rep Rows 3–6 for patt throughout Back and Front. Work even in patt for 10 (12, 14, 16, 18) more, changing colors every 2 rows as established.

Shape Armhole

Next Row: Sl st in next 5 (6, 6, 6, 7) sts, ch 1, working in rem unused lps 2 rows below, hdc in each st across to the last 5 (6, 6, 6, 7) sts, turn, leaving rem sts unworked, turn—28 (30, 32, 34, 36) hdc.

Work even in established patt for 15 (17, 19, 21, 23) more rows.

Last Row: Ch 1, working in rem unused lps 2 rows below, dc in next 10 (10, 11, 12, 12) sts, sl st in next 8 (10, 10, 10, 12) sts, dc in last 10 (10, 11, 12, 12) sts. Fasten off.

LEFT FRONT

With A, ch 21 (23, 24, 25, 27).

Row 1 (RS): Hdc in 3rd ch from hook and in each ch across, turn—19 (21, 22, 23, 25) hdc.

Work same as back to Shape Armhole.

Next Row: Ch 1, working in rem unused lps 2 rows below, hdc in each st across to the last 5 (6, 6, 6, 7) sts, turn, leaving rem sts unworked, turn—14 (15, 16, 17, 18) hdc.

Work even in established patt for 15 (17, 19, 21, 23) more rows.

Last Row: Ch 1, working in rem unused lps 2 rows below, hdc in next 4 (5, 5, 5, 6) sts, hdc in last 10 (10, 11, 12, 12) sts. Fasten off.

Edging

Row 1: With WS facing, join A with a sc in first row-end st on Left Front edge, sc in each row-end st across to top corner, complete last st with C, turn—33 (37, 41, 45, 49) sc.

Row 2: Ch 1, sc in each st across. Fasten off C.

RIGHT FRONT

Work same as Left Front to Shape Armhole.

Next Row: Working in rem unused lps 2 rows below, sl st in next 5 (6, 6, 6, 7) sts, ch 1, hdc in each st across, turn—14 (15, 16, 17, 18) hdc.

Work even in established patt for 15 (17, 19, 21, 23) more rows.

Last Row: Ch 1, working in rem unused lps 2 rows below, hdc in next 10 (10, 11, 12, 12) sts, hdc in last 4 (5, 5, 5, 6) sts. Fasten off.

Edging

Row 1: With WS facing, join A with a sc in top row-end st on Right Front edge, sc in each row-end st across to bottom corner, complete last st with C, turn—33 (37, 41, 45, 49) sc.

Row 2: Ch 1, sc in each st across. Fasten off C.

SLEEVES (MAKE 2)

Note: *These are set-in sleeves, starting at wrist and working toward shoulder.*

Starting at cuff edge with B, ch 31 (33, 35, 37, 39).

Row 1: Hdc in 3rd ch from hook and in each ch across, turn—29 (31, 33, 35, 37) hdc.

Row 2: Ch 2, hdc in each st across, turn.

Rows 3–26 (28, 30, 32, 34): Rep Row 2.

Shape Cap

Row 1: Working in rem unused lps 2 rows below, sl st in next 5 (6, 6, 6, 7) sts, ch 2 (does not count as a st here and throughout), hdc in each st across to last 5 (6, 6, 6, 7) sts, turn, leave rem sts unworked—19 (19, 21, 23, 23) hdc.

Rows 2–3: Ch 2, hdc in first hdc, hdc in each hdc across, turn.

Row 4 (dec row): Ch 2, hdc in same st, hdc2tog over next 2 sts, hdc in each st across to last 3 sts, hdc2tog over next 2 sts, hdc in last st, turn—17 (17, 19, 21, 21) hdc.

Dec 1 hdc at each end of every 3rd row twice, then at each end of every row 3 (3, 4, 5, 5) more times—7 hdc at end of last row.

Fasten off.

HOOD

Starting at bottom edge with C, ch 50 (52, 56, 58, 62).

Row 1: Hdc in 3rd ch from hook and in each ch across, turn—48 (50, 54, 56, 60) hdc.

Rows 2–21 (23, 27, 29, 33): Ch 2, hdc in first hdc, hdc in each hdc across, turn. Fasten off leaving an 18" (45.5 cm) sewing length—48 (50, 54, 56, 60) hdc.

Pin all pieces and block to measurements

SWEATER ASSEMBLY

With yarn needle and matching yarn, whipstitch shoulder seams, matching stitches.

Line up last row of sleeve cap, straddle it over the shoulder seam, whipstitch it in place. Working from underarm to cuff edge, whipstitch sleeve seam. Whipstitch side seams from hem to underarm. Sew other sleeve and side seam in same manner.

Hood

Excluding front edging rows, align bottom edge of hood with the last rows of Left Front, Back neck edge, and Right Front, easing in fullness across back neck section. Whipstitch the hood in place.

Hood Assembly

With yarn needle and sewing length, fold hood in half so that the first st and the last st meet, matching sts, whipstitch a seam along last row of Hood toward the fold. Fasten off.

(continued)

HOODIE SCHEMATICS

3¼ (3¼, 3½, 4, 4)"
(8.25 [8.25, 8.75, 10, 10] cm)

3½ (3½, 3½, 3½, 4)"
(8.75 [8.75, 8.75, 8.75, 10] cm)

4¼ (4¾, 5¼, 5¾, 6¼)"
(10.75 [12, 13.25, 14.75, 16] cm)

BACK

4 (4½, 5, 5½, 6)"
(10 [11.25, 12.75, 14, 15.25] cm)

13¼ (14, 14½, 15½, 16½)"
(33.75 [35.25, 36.5, 39.25, 41.75] cm)

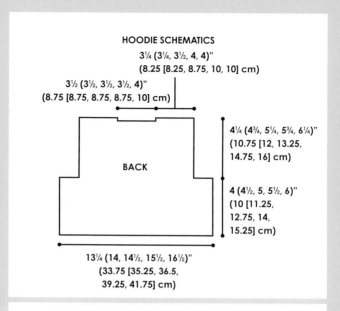

HOODIE SCHEMATICS

4¾ (4¾, 5, 5½, 5½)"
(12 [12, 12.75, 14, 14] cm)

SLEEVE

9½ (10, 11, 11½, 12½)"
(24.25 [25.5, 28, 29.25, 31.75] cm)

9½ (10¼, 11, 11½, 12¼)"
(24.25 [26.25, 28, 29.25, 31.25] cm)

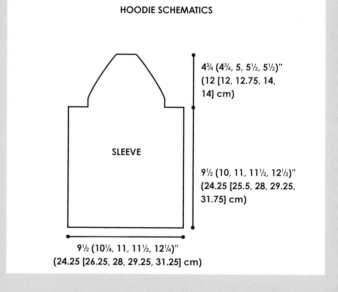

FINISHING

Hood Edging

Row 1: With RS facing, join C with a sc in front edge of Hood at right front, sc in each row-end st across front edge of Hood, changing to A in last st, turn—42 (46, 54, 58, 66) hdc.

Row 2: Ch 2, hdc in flo of each st across, changing to B in last st, turn.

Row 3: Ch 1, using the unused lps of Row 1, sc in first st, (ch 3, sc) in each st across. Fasten off.

Sweater Edging

Row 1: With RS facing, join C with a sc at top of left front edge, sc in each sc across to corner, 3 sc in corner, sc evenly across bottom edge to next corner, 3 sc in corner st, sc in each st across right front edge, turn.

Row 2: Ch 1, sc in each sc across. Fasten off C.

Cuff Edging

Rnd 1: With RS facing, join B with a sl st in any st on cuff edge of one Sleeve, ch 1, (sl st, ch 1) in each st around, no need to join. Fasten off B.

Rep Cuff Edging around other Sleeve.

Ties (Make 2)

With B, ch 30 (30, 32, 32, 34). Fasten off, leaving 6" (15 cm) tail.

Join A to back bar of last ch, sl st in back bar of each ch across. Fasten off.

With 6" (15 cm) tail and yarn needle, sew 1 Tie where hood meets the front corner on each side. Tie an overhand knot in the dangling yarn ends and trim the tails to match each other in length.

Weave in ends.

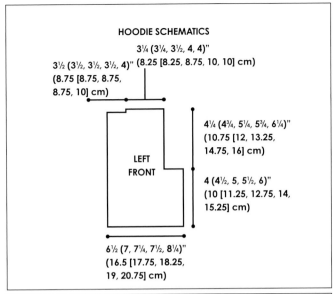

HOODIE SCHEMATICS

3¼ (3¼, 3½, 4, 4)" (8.25 [8.25, 8.75, 10, 10] cm)

3½ (3½, 3½, 3½, 4)" (8.75 [8.75, 8.75, 8.75, 10] cm)

LEFT FRONT

4¼ (4¾, 5¼, 5¾, 6¼)" (10.75 [12, 13.25, 14.75, 16] cm)

4 (4½, 5, 5½, 6)" (10 [11.25, 12.75, 14, 15.25] cm)

6½ (7, 7¼, 7½, 8¼)" (16.5 [17.75, 18.25, 19, 20.75] cm)

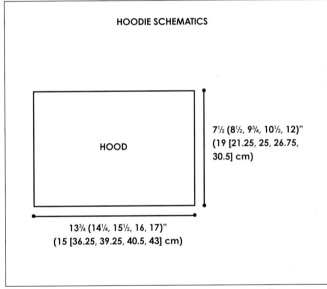

HOODIE SCHEMATICS

HOOD

7½ (8½, 9¾, 10½, 12)" (19 [21.25, 25, 26.75, 30.5] cm)

13¾ (14¼, 15½, 16, 17)" (15 [36.25, 39.25, 40.5, 43] cm)

Plated Steel Tunisian T-Shirt

This wash-and-wear cotton shirt is as rugged as he is. With just a hint of texture, and classy neutrals, this slouchy T will have the casual style he craves. Even if he is the strong and silent type, this t-shirt will speak volumes with a cool, confident attitude.

Special Stitches Used

- **twisted simple stitch (Tws)**
  Insert hook from left to right (right to left for left-handers) under front vertical bar of next stitch, yo, draw up lp.

- **standard return pass**
  Yo, draw through 1 lp on hook, *yo, draw through 2 lps on hook, rep from * until 1 lp remains on hook.

- **special return pass**
  Yo, draw through one lp on hook, *yo, draw through 2 lps on hook, rep from * across until 2 lps remain, yo with B, and pull through last two lps on hook. (One lp remains on hook and it is color B).

- **Tss2tog (dec)**
  Tunisian simple stitch two together. Insert hook under next two vertical bars at the same time as if to work Tunisian Simple St, yo, pull up a lp.

- **twisted simple bind off (Tws bind off)**
  (Work a forward pass only to complete the final row). Skip first vertical bar, *Tws in next vertical bar and draw up a lp, draw that loop also through the lp on the hook, rep from * across to last st, draw up a lp in last vertical bar, yo and pull through both lps on hook. Fasten off.

- **single crochet 2 together (sc2tog)**
  [Insert hook in next st, yo, draw yarn through st] twice, yo, draw yarn through 3 lps on hook.

Skill Level
Intermediate

Finished Size
Directions are given for boy's size 4. Changes for 6, 8, 10, and 12 are in parentheses.

Finished Chest: 28 (29½, 31, 33, 34½)" (71 [75, 79, 84, 87.5] cm)

Finished Length: 14 (15, 16, 17, 18)" (35.5 [38, 40.5, 43, 45.5] cm)

Gauge
19 sts and 16 rows in Tws patt = 4" (10 cm). Take time to check gauge.

Yarn
2

Rowan Cotton Glace, 100% cotton, 3 oz (50 g)/125 yd (115 cm): 5 (6, 6, 7, 8) balls #831 Dawn Grey (A) and 1 ball #727 Black (B)

Tools
H/8 (5 mm) crochet hook

H/8 (5 mm) 14" (35.5 cm) Tunisian/ Afghan crochet hook

yarn needle

Notes: *RS is always facing in this Tunisian pattern. One row consists of a forward pass and a return pass.*

BACK

With A, and Afghan hook, ch 66 (70, 74, 78, 82).

Row 1 (RS): Fwd Pass: Working in back bar of ch sts, pull up a loop in 2nd ch from hook and in each ch across—66 (70, 74, 78, 82) lps on hook.

Return Pass: Work standard return pass.

Row 2: Fwd Pass: Skip first vertical bar, here and on each row, Twisted simple st (Tws) in each vertical bar across to last vertical bar, draw up a lp in last vertical bar.

Return Pass: Yo, draw through one lp on hook, *yo, draw through 2 lps on hook, rep from * across until 2 lps remain, yo with B, and pull through last two lps on hook. (One lp remains on hook and it is color B).

Row 3: Fwd Pass: With B, skip first vertical bar, Tws in each vertical bar across to last vertical bar, draw up a lp in last vertical bar.

Return Pass: Drop B, yo with A, pull through one lp on hook, *yo and pull through 2 lps on hook, rep from * across until there is one lp on hook.

Rows 4–48 (51, 54, 57, 60): Fwd Pass: Skip first vertical bar, here and on each row, Tws in each vertical bar across to last vertical bar, draw up a loop in last vertical bar.

Return Pass: Work standard return pass.

Do not fasten off, continue to shoulder and neck shaping.

Right Shoulder/Neck Shaping

Row 1: Fwd Pass: Skip first vertical bar, Tws in next 22 (23, 25, 26, 28) sts, leave remaining sts unworked—23 (24, 26, 27, 29) lps on hook.

Return Pass: Work standard return pass. PM in this row to mark it as Row 1.

Row 2 (dec row): Fwd Pass: Skip first vertical bar, tws in each st across to last 5 sts, [tss2tog in next 2 sts] twice, draw up a lp in last vertical bar.

Return Pass: Work standard return pass—21 (22, 24, 25, 27) sts.

Rep this dec every other row 2 (3, 3, 4, 4) more times, then every row 1 (0, 1, 0, 1) more time—15 (16, 16, 17, 17) sts at end of last row.

Next Row: Work Tws bind off across. (See Special Stitches).

Left Shoulder/Neck Shaping

Row 1: Fwd Pass: Skip 20 (22, 22, 24, 24) sts at center neck, join new yarn by bringing up a lp of A in next st (lp on hook counts as the first st), Tws in each vertical bar across, draw up a lp in last vertical bar—23 (24, 26, 27, 29) sts.

Return Pass: Work standard return pass.

Row 2 (dec row): Fwd Pass: Skip first vertical bar, [tss2tog in next 2 sts] twice, Tws in each st across, draw up a loop in last vertical bar.

Return Pass: Work standard return pass—21 (22, 24, 25, 27) sts.

Rep this dec every other row 2 (3, 3, 4, 4) more times, then every row 1 (0, 1, 0, 1) more time—15 (16, 16, 17, 17) sts.

Next Row: Work Tws bind off across.

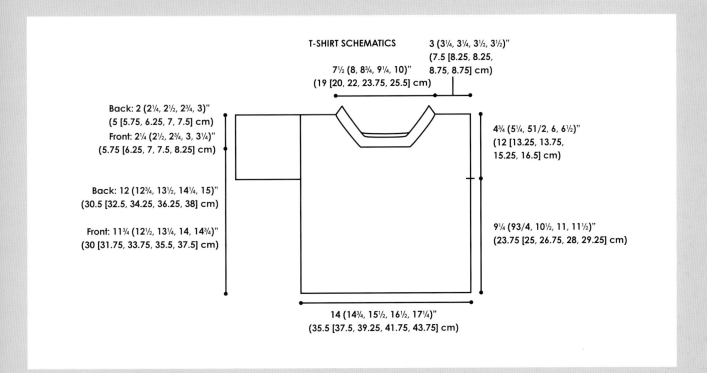

T-SHIRT SCHEMATICS

3 (3¼, 3¼, 3½, 3½)"
(7.5 [8.25, 8.25, 8.75, 8.75] cm)

7½ (8, 8¾, 9¼, 10)"
(19 [20, 22, 23.75, 25.5] cm)

Back: 2 (2¼, 2½, 2¾, 3)"
(5 [5.75, 6.25, 7, 7.5] cm)
Front: 2¼ (2½, 2¾, 3, 3¼)"
(5.75 [6.25, 7, 7.5, 8.25] cm)

4¾ (5¼, 51/2, 6, 6½)"
(12 [13.25, 13.75, 15.25, 16.5] cm)

Back: 12 (12¾, 13½, 14¼, 15)"
(30.5 [32.5, 34.25, 36.25, 38] cm)

Front: 11¾ (12½, 13¼, 14, 14¾)"
(30 [31.75, 33.75, 35.5, 37.5] cm)

9¼ (93/4, 10½, 11, 11½)"
(23.75 [25, 26.75, 28, 29.25] cm)

14 (14¾, 15½, 16½, 17¼)"
(35.5 [37.5, 39.25, 41.75, 43.75] cm)

FRONT

Work same as back through Row 47 (50, 53, 56, 59).

Left Shoulder/Neck Shaping

Row 1: Fwd Pass: Skip first vertical bar, Tws in next 22 (23, 25, 26, 28) sts, leave remaining sts un-worked—23 (24, 26, 27, 29) loops on hook.

Return Pass: Work standard return pass. PM in this row to mark it as Row 1.

Row 2 (dec row): Fwd Pass: Skip first vertical bar, tws in each st across to last 5 sts, [tss2tog in next 2 sts] twice, draw up a loop in last vertical bar.

Return Pass: Work standard return pass—21 (22, 24, 25, 27) sts.

Rep this dec every other row 3 (3, 4, 4, 5) more times, then work 0 (1, 0, 1, 0) row even—15 (16, 16, 17, 17) sts.

Next Row: Work Tws bind off across.

Right Shoulder/Neck Shaping

Row 1: Fwd Pass: Skip 20 [22, 22, 24, 24] sts at center neck, join new yarn by bringing up a lp of A in next st (lp on hook counts as the first st), Tws in each vertical bar across, draw up a lp in last vertical bar—23 (24, 26, 27, 29) sts.

Return Pass: Work standard return pass.

Row 2 (dec row): Fwd Pass: Skip first vertical bar, [tss2tog in next 2 sts] twice, Tws in each st across, draw up a lp in last vertical bar.

Return Pass: Work standard return pass—21 (22, 24, 25, 27) sts.

Rep this dec every other row 3 (3, 4, 4, 5) more times, then work 0 (1, 0, 1, 0) row even—15 (16, 16, 17, 17) sts.

Next Row: Work Tws bind off across.

(continued)

SLEEVES (MAKE 2)

Starting at cuff edge, with A, and Afghan hook, ch 46 (50, 54, 58, 62).

Row 1 (RS): Fwd Pass: Working in back bar of ch sts, pull up a lp in 2nd ch from hook and in each ch across—46 (50, 54, 58, 62) lps on hook.

Return Pass: Work standard return pass.

Row 2: Fwd Pass: Skip first vertical bar, here and on each row, Twisted simple st (Tws) in each vertical bar across to last vertical bar, draw up a loop in last vertical bar.

Return Pass: Yo, draw through one lp on hook, *yo, draw through 2 lps on hook, rep from * across until 2 lps remain, yo with B, and pull through last two lps on hook. (One lp remains on hook and it is color B).

Row 3: Fwd Pass: With B, skip first vertical bar, Tws in each vertical bar across to last vertical bar, draw up a lp in last vertical bar.

Return Pass: Drop B, yo with A, pull through one lp on hook, *yo and pull through 2 lps on hook, rep from * across until there is one lp on hook.

Rows 4–21 (22, 23, 24, 25): Fwd Pass: Skip first vertical bar, here and on each row, Tws in each vertical bar across to last vertical bar, draw up a loop in last vertical bar.

Return Pass: Work standard return pass.

Next Row: Work Tws bind off across.

Block all pieces to measurements.

ASSEMBLY

With matching yarn and yarn needle, and matching stitches, mattress stitch the shoulder seams.

Fold Sleeve in half lengthwise. Matching fold of top edge of Sleeve to shoulder seam, and with A and yarn needle, mattress stitch the Sleeve in place. With A, sew side seams from hem to underarm. Sew sleeve seam from sleeve edge to under arm.

Repeat for other Sleeve and side seams.

FINISHING

Hem Edgings

Rnd 1: With RS facing, and standard crochet hook, join A with sc at side seam on bottom edge, sc in each st around, join with a sl st in first sc, turn.

Rnd 2 (WS): Sl st in each sc around (on wrong side of the fabric to combat curling). Fasten off.

Sleeve Edgings

Rnd 1: With RS facing, and standard crochet hook, join A with sc at side seam on cuff edge of one Sleeve, sc in each st around, join with a sl st in first sc, turn.

Rnd 2 (WS): Sl st in each sc around (worked on WS of fabric to combat curling). Fasten off.

Rep Sleeve Edging on other Sleeve.

Neck edging

Rnd 1: With RS facing, and standard crochet hook, join A with sc in first row-end st to the left one shoulder seam, *sc in each row-end st across neck shaping to last row before neck shaping, work Tws bind off across center 20 (22, 22, 24, 24) sts, sc in each row-end st across to next shoulder seam, rep from * once, join with a sl st in first sc. PM at beg and end of each Tws section—74 (82, 86, 94, 98) sc.

Rnd 2: Ch 1, sc in each st around, working sc2tog at each marker, join with sl st in first sc. Move marker up each rnd—70 (78, 82, 90, 94) sc.

Rnds 3–5: Rep Rnd 2—58 (66, 70, 78, 82) sts at end of last rnd.

TURN after round 5.

Rnd 6 (WS): With WS facing, sl st in each st around. Fasten off.

Appliqué

With A, ch 6.

Row 1: Fwd Pass: Pull up a lp in 2nd ch from hook and in next 4 chs--6 lps on hook.

Reurn Pass: Yo with B and pull through 2 lps on hook across until one lp remains.

Row 2: Fwd Pass: With B, skip first vertical lp, tss in each st across.

Return Pass: Return Pass with A.

Row 3: Fwd Pass: With A, skip first vertical loop, tss in each st across.

Return Pass: Return Pass with B.

Row 4: Rep Row 2.

Row 5: Rep Row 3.

Row 6: With B, place 3 sc in each corner, 3 sc along each side, join with sl st in first sc—24 sc.

Row 7: With A, sc in each st around, fasten off leaving a long tail for sewing.

Orient the motif sideways and sew it onto left front shoulder.

Shady Lady Hat

There is nothing better than having a child wear and love something that was handmade. Made of lightweight cotton yarns, this breathable hat will keep her covered and cool. Perfect for the stylish little girl who wants to look great but wants to sport something a little different than a flowered topper. This hat has all the style without the frill. If your girly-girl wants to be even more of a trendsetter, swap out the pink for her signature color.

Special Stitches Used

- **3 double crochet cluster (3dcCL)**
  [Yo, insert hook in next sp, yo, draw yarn through sp, yo, draw yarn through 2 lps on hook] 3 times in same sp, yo, draw yarn through 4 lps on hook.

- **beginning 3 double crochet cluster (beg 3dcCL)**
  Ch 3, [yo, insert hook in next sp, yo, draw yarn through sp, yo, draw yarn through 2 lps on hook] 3 times in same sp, yo, draw yarn through 3 lps on hook.

Skill Level
Intermediate

Finished Size
Circumference: 18" (45.5 cm)

Gauge
First 4 rnds = 4" (10 cm) in diameter.
Take time to check gauge.

Yarn

4

Nazli Gelin Garden 3, 100% Egyptian Giza Mercerized Cotton, 1.76 oz (50 g)/136 yd (124 m): 1 ball each #06 Pink (A) and #01 White (B)

Tools
F/5 (3.75 mm) crochet hook
yarn needle

Notes: All rounds are worked from RS without turning. Rounds are joined as specified.

HAT

With A, form an adjustable ring (page 15).

Rnd 1 (RS): Ch 3 (counts as dc), 9 dc in ring, tighten ring, join with a sl st in top beg ch-3—10 dc.

Rnd 2: Ch 1, (sc, ch 3) in each dc around, join with a sl st in first sc—10 sc, 10 ch-3 sps.

Rnd 3: Sl st in first ch-3 sp, beg 3dcCL in first sp, *ch 3, 3dcCL in next ch-3 sp, rep from * around, ch 3, join with a sl st in top of beg 3dcCL—10 3dcCL; 10 ch-3 sps.

Rnd 4: Ch 1, (sc, ch 5, sc) in first st, *3 sc in ch-3 sp, (sc, ch 5, sc) in next 3dcCL, rep from * around, 3 sc in last ch-3 sp, join with a sl st in first sc—10 ch-5 lps, 50 sc.

Rnd 5: Sl st in next ch-5 sp, (beg 3dcCL, ch 3, 3dcCL) in same sp, *ch 3, sk next 2 sc, sc in next sc, sk next 2 sc, ch 3**, (3dcCL, ch 3, 3dcCL) in next ch-5 sp, rep from * around, ending last rep at **, join with a sl st in top of beg 3dcCL.

Rnd 6: Sl st in next ch-3 sp, (beg 3dcCL, ch 3, 3dcCL) in same ch-3 sp, *ch 1, sk next ch-3 sp, tr in next sc, ch 1, sk next ch-3 sp**, (3dcCL, ch 3, 3dcCL) in next ch-3 sp, rep from * around, ending last rep at **, join with a sl st in top of beg 3dcCL—20 3dcCL; 10 tr.

Rnd 7: Sl st in next ch-3 sp, (beg 3dcCL, ch 3, 3dcCL) in same ch-3 sp, *ch 1, 3dcCL in tr, ch 1**, (3dcCL, ch 3, 3dcCL) in ch-3 sp, rep from * around, ending last rep at **, join with a sl st in top of beg 3dcCL—30 3dcCL; 10 ch-3 sps.

Begin Sides

Rnds 8–13: Sl st in next ch-3 sp, (beg 3dcCL, ch 3, 3dcCL) in same ch-3 sp, *ch 1, 3dcCL in CL, ch 1**, (3dcCL, ch 3, 3dcCL) in ch-3 sp, rep from * around, ending last rep at **, join with a sl st in top of beg 3dcCL.

Rnd 14: Working in flo of sts, ch 2 (counts as hdc here and throughout), hdc in each st and ch around, join with a sl st in top of beg ch-2—80 hdc.

Rnd 15: Working in both lps of sts, ch 2, hdc in next 2 sts, 2 hdc in next st, *hdc in next 3 sts, 2 hdc in next st, rep from * around, join with a sl st in top beg ch-2—100 hdc.

Rnd 16: Ch 2, hdc in next 3 sts, 2 hdc in next st, *hdc in next 4 sts, 2 hdc in next st, rep from * around, join with a sl st in top beg ch-2—120 hdc.

Rnds 17–19: Ch 2, hdc in each st around, join with a sl st in top beg ch-2. Fasten off A.

Rnd 20: With RS facing, join B with a sl st in any st, sl st in each st around. Fasten off B.

POLKA DOTS

Large Dot

With A, ch 4, sl st in first st to form a ring.

Rnd 1: Work Beg 3dcCL in ring, ch 4, [3dcCL, ch 4] 4 times in ring, join with a sl st in first 3dcCL—5 3dcCL, 5 ch-4 sps). Fasten off A.

Rnd 2: With RS facing, join B with a sc in any ch-4 sp, 3 more sc in same sp, sc in next CL, *4 sc in ch-4 sp, sc in next CL, rep from * around, join with a sl st in first sc—25 sc. Fasten off B.

Small Dot

With A, ch 4, sl st in first st to form a ring.

Rnd 1: Ch 1, work 6 sc in ring, join with a sl st in first sc—6 sc.

Rnd 2: Ch 2 (counts as hdc), hdc in same st, 2 hdc in each st around, join with a sl st in top of beg ch-2—12 hdc. Fasten off A.

Rnd 3: With RS facing, join B with a sc in any hdc, ch 1, (sc, ch 1) in each st around, join with a sl st in first sc—12 ch-1 sps. Fasten off B.

With yarn needle and A, sew polka dots onto hat as pictured.

chapter 5

Accessorize

Whimsical Wheels Necklace and Ring

This delightful combination of embroidery-embellished wheels and petite slip stitch ribbons, will brighten any girl's day. A ring can also be made with just one wheel, and a band that is just her size.

Special Stitches Used

- *Invisible Fasten Off (page 14)*
  Cut the yarn, leaving a 3" (7.5 cm) tail. Insert the hook into the blo of the first st in rnd, yo, and pull the yarn all the way through the loop on the hook, as if to fasten off in the usual way. Insert the hook in both lps of next st, yo with tail end and pull through st. Finally, insert the hook in the flo of last st in rnd, yo, pull yarn down through.

Skill Level
Easy

Finished Measurement
16½" (42 cm) from end to end, including the Fastening Loop.

Gauge
Small Wheel = 1¼" (3 cm) in diameter

Large Wheel = 1½" (4 mm) in diameter

31 sts = 4" (10 cm) in ribbon pattern

Yarn

Berroco Weekend DK, 75% acrylic, 25% Peruvian cotton, 268 yd (245 m)/3.5 oz (100 g): 1 skein each #2972 Marigold (A), #2955 Reddy (B), and #2923 Tomatillo (C)

Tools
C/2 (2.75 mm) crochet hook

D/3 (3.25 mm) crochet hook

E/4 (3.50 mm) crochet hook

yarn needle

sewing needle

invisible nylon thread

rust-proof pins

SMALL WHEEL

Make 1 each using B and C for 2nd color.

With D/3 (3.25mm) hook and A, make a Magic Ring.

Rnd 1: Insert hook in ring, yo and pull up a lp, ch 2, work 7 hdc in ring, join with a sl st in first hdc. Pull on tail end of yarn to close ring.

Rnd 2: Ch 1, sc in same st, 2 sc in each st around, join with sl st in first sc—13 sts. Fasten off A, join 2nd color.

Rnd 3: With 2nd color, ch 1, sc in each st around, join with a sl st in first sc. Invisible Fasten Off.

Rnd 4: Working with RS facing you, surface crochet in sts from Rnd 2 by inserting hook in a st from front of work to back, holding yarn on back of work, yo, pull up a lp, *insert hook in next st in Rnd 2, yo, draw up a lp, then pull this lp through lp already on hook, rep from * around. Pull the tail end of the yarn up to the top surface of your work then work an Invisible Fasten Off.

Rnd 5: Working in the sts formed in Rnd 4, ch 2 (counts as hdc), hdc in each st around, join with a sl st in top of beg ch 2.

Rnd 6: Note: *This rnd will join Rnds 3 and 5 together.* *Insert hook in next st and in corresponding st in Rnd 3, work a sl st, rep from * around. Cut the yarn, leaving a 3" (7.5 cm) tail. Pull the tail end of the yarn up to the top surface of your work then work an Invisible Fasten Off.

LARGE WHEEL

Make 1 each using B and C for 2nd color.

With E/4 (3.50 mm) and A, make a Magic Ring.

Rnd 1: Yo and draw up a lp, ch 2, work 8 hdc in ring, join with a sl st in first hdc. Pull on tail end of yarn to close ring.

Rnd 2: Ch 1, sc in same st, 2 sc in each st around, join with al st in first sc—15 sts). Fasten off A, join 2nd color.

Rnds 3–6: Rep rnds 3–6 of Small Wheel.

RIBBONS

Middle Ribbon (left)

With C/2 (2.75 mm) hook and A, ch 3.

Rnd 1: Work 7 hdc in the 3rd ch from hook, join with a sl st in first hdc.

Rnd 2: [Sl st in next st, sk 1 st] 3 times–Fastening Dome made.

Row 3: Ch 75, working in blo of ch sts, sl st in 2nd ch from hook and in each ch across. Fasten off.

Outer Ribbon (left)

With C/2 (2.75 mm) hook join C with a sl st in the Middle Ribbon (right) in the blo of the st at the base of the Fastening Dome, ch 75, working in blo of ch sts, sl st in 2nd ch from hook and in each ch across. Fasten off.

Inner Ribbon (left)

With C/2 (2.75 mm) hook join B with a sl st in the Middle Ribbon (right) in the blo of the st at the base of the Fastening Dome, ch 75, working in blo of ch sts, sl st in 2nd ch from hook and in each ch across. Fasten off.

Middle Ribbon (right)

With C/2 (2.75 mm) hook and A, ch 84, working in blo of ch sts, sl st in 2nd ch from hook and in each ch across. Fasten off. The Fastening Loop was formed at the end of this Ribbon.

Outer Ribbon (right)

With C/2 (2.75 mm) hook and B, ch 75, then remove lp from hook and insert hook in the Middle Ribbon in the flo of the st at the base of the Fastening Loop and put the Outer Ribbon ch lp back on hook. Pull the Outer Ribbon lp through the Middle Ribbon lp. Working in blo of ch sts, sl st in 2nd ch from hook and in each ch across. Fasten off.

Inner Ribbon (right)

With C/2 (2.75 mm) hook, join C in the Middle Ribbon in the blo of the st at the base of the Fastening Loop, ch 75, sl st in 2nd ch from hook and in each ch across. Fasten off.

FINISHING

With yarn needle and B, embroider a star in the
middle of each Wheel made in yarn C as follows:
Thread yarn on needle, * bring needle up through
center of Wheel, insert needle down through
in top of any st in Rnd 1, rep from * in each sts
around. In same manner, with C, embroider a
star in the middle of each Wheel made in yarn B.
Weave in ends. Pin the 4 Wheels together, forming a semicircle. Alternate colors and place the
Large Wheels in the center, flanked by a Small
Wheel on each side. With a sewing needle and
invisible nylon thread, sew the Wheels together
where they meet. Holding all three Ribbons
together, aligning ends, tie an overhand knot at
the end of left and right Ribbon clusters leaving
a 1½" (4 cm) tail. Pin each knot to the top of their
respective Wheels. Sew them to the Wheels with
invisible thread. Pin necklace into desired shape
on a blocking board and wet or steam block.

WHEEL RING

Follow instructions to make a Small Wheel in desired colors, and embroider a star in the middle as
before. With C/2 (2.75 mm) hook, use the same
yarn color you used for Rnds 3–6, and working
on the WS of the Small Wheel, insert hook in a
horizontal lp of a st from Rnd 1, yo and draw up
a lp, ch 14, sl st in a horizontal lp of a st from rnd
1 that is directly across from where yarn is joined,
sl st in back bar of each ch across. Fasten off.
Weave in ends.

Charming Bracelet

Every girl should have a charm bracelet, and this dainty, heart-themed bracelet embellished with pearls is sure to be a favorite in her jewelry collection. Light-weight cotton thread is comfortable to wear and gives great detail and definition to the motifs. More links can easily be added to the bracelet, if you are tempted to make one for yourself!

Special Stitches Used

- *Invisible Fasten Off (page 14)*
  Cut yarn leaving a 3" (7.5 cm) tail. Insert hook in blo of first st in rnd, yo, and draw yarn all the way through the lp on the hook, as if to fasten off in the usual way. Insert the hook in both lps of next st, yo with tail end and pull through st. Finally, insert hook in flo of last st in rnd, yo, draw yarn down through.

- *picot*
  After making the indicated number of ch sts, sl st in both the flo and left vertical leg of last sc made, to form a picot.

- *popcorn*
  Work 6 dc in designated st, drop lp from hook, insert hook in first dc, place dropped lp back on hook and draw through dc.

Skill Level
Intermediate

Finished Measurement
6" (15 cm) long from end to end

Gauge
Large Links = ⅞" (2.2 cm) wide x ¾" (2 cm) tall; Small Charms = ⅞" (2.2 cm) wide x ¾" (2 cm) tall; Medium Charms = 1⅜" (3.5 cm) wide x 1¼" (3.2 cm) tall; Large Charm = 1⅝" (4 cm) wide x 1⅜" (3.5 cm) tall.

Thread

Universal Yarn Garden 10, 100% Egyptian Giza Mercerized Cotton, 308 yd (282 m)/1.75 oz (50 g): 1 ball each #700-04 (A), #700-39 (B), #700-31 (C)

Tools
size 7 (1.5 mm) steel crochet hook
yarn needle
sewing needle
one 5-mm pearl
two 3-mm pearls
invisible nylon thread

LARGE LINKS (MAKE 6)

With A, make a Magic Ring (page 15).

Rnd 1: Insert hook in ring, yo and pull up a lp, ch 1, work 18 sc in ring, join with a sl st in first sc.

Rnd 2: Working over sts in Rnd 1, work 23 hdc in center ring. Invisible Fasten Off.

Note: After one Large Link has been completed, use it as a size guide for the rem five. The size of each link can be adjusted by tightening or loosening the Magic Ring. Weave in ends.

CONNECTING LINKS (MAKE 6)

With A, ch 15. Pick up 2 Large Links, insert ch into the links and working the back bar of ch sts, being careful not to twist ch, sl st in first ch to form a ring, linking the two Large Links together, ch 1, sc in each ch around. Invisible Fasten Off. Rep these instructions, twice more. You will now have three sets of joined Large Links. Make one more Connecting Link on the end of one of the sets. This Connecting Link will become the Fastening Loop. Next, join the three sets of Large Links together with Connecting Links.

SMALL CHARM (MAKE 3)

With B, make a Magic Ring.

Rnd 1: Insert the hook into the ring, yo and draw up a lp, ch 2, (3 tr, 4 dc, tr, 4 dc, 3 tr, ch 2, sl st) in ring. Pull on tail of yarn to close ring. Fasten off B, join A in first st.

Rnd 2: With A, work 2 sc in next ch-2 sp, 2 sc in each of next 2 sts, sc in each of next 5 sts, (sc, hdc, sc) in next st, sc in each of next 5 sts, 2 sc in each of next 2 sts, 2 sc in next ch-2 sp, sl st in ring. Fasten off A.

MEDIUM CHARM (MAKE 2)

With B, make a Magic Ring.

Rnd 1: Insert hook into ring, yo and draw up a lp, ch 3, work 5 dc in designated st, drop lp from hook, insert hook in top of beg ch-3, place dropped lp back on hook and draw through st (beg popcorn made), *ch 3, popcorn in ring, rep from * twice, ch 3, join with a sl st in beg popcorn. Pull on tail end of yarn to close ring. Fasten off B, join A in first st.

Rnd 2: With A, ch 1, sl st in first ch sp, ch 5, (3 dc, ch 3, dc, hdc) in next ch sp, ch 3, (hdc, ch 3, hdc) in next ch-3 sp, ch 3, (hdc, dc, ch 3, 3 dc) in next ch-3 sp, ch 5, join with a sl st first sl st.

Rnd 3: *Note: When instruction refers to sts, each ch in a ch sp counts as one st.* (Sc, [2 sc, ch-2 picot] twice) in first ch-5 sp, *sc in next 2 sts, ch-2 picot, rep from * 5 times, (2 sc, ch 3 picot, sc) in next ch-3 sp, **Sc in next st, ch 2 picot, sc in next st, rep from ** 7 times, sc in same ch-5 sp, join with a sl st in first sl st at beg of rnd. Fasten off A.

LARGE CHARM (MAKE 1)

With B, make a Magic Ring.

Rnd 1: Rep Rnd 1 of Medium Charm. Fasten off B, join A in first st.

Rnd 2: With A, ch 1, sl st into first ch-5 sp, ch 6, (3 tr, ch 3, tr, dc) in next ch sp, ch 2, (2 dc, ch 3, 2 dc) in next ch-3 sp, ch 2, (dc, tr, ch 3, 3 tr) in next ch-3 sp, ch 6, join with a sl st in first st st.

Rnd 3: *Note: When instruction refers to sts, each ch in a ch sp counts as one st.* (2 sc, ch-3 picot) 3 times in next ch-6 sp, *sc in each of next 2 sts, ch-3 picot, rep from * 5 times, (2 sc, ch-4 picot, sc) in next ch-3 sp, **sc in next st, ch-3 picot sc, sc in next st, rep from ** 8 times, join with a sl st in first sl st. Fasten off A.

SMALL CHARM CONNECTING LINKS

With C, ch 13.

Pick up a Small Charm and insert ch into the center of the Small Charm, and into the second Large Link (2 Links from the Fastening Loop) and being careful not to twist ch, sl st in back bar of first ch to form a ring, linking the Small Charm and Large Link together, ch 1, working in back bar of sts, sc in each ch around. Invisible Fasten Off. Rep these instructions to attach Small Charms to the 4th and 6th Large Links.

MEDIUM CHARM CONNECTING LINKS

With C, ch 15.

Pick up a Medium Charm and insert ch into the ch sp that is behind the top two petals of the flower, and into the First Large Link (next to the Fastening Loop) and being careful not to twist ch, sl st in back bar of first ch to form a ring, linking the Medium Charm and Large Link together, ch 1, working in back bar of sts, sc in each ch around. Invisible Fasten Off. Rep these instructions in the 5th Large Link.

LARGE CHARM CONNECTING LINK

With C, ch 15.

Pick up the Large Charm and insert ch into the ch sp that is behind the top two petals of the flower, and into the Third Large Link and being careful not to twist ch, sl st in back bar of first ch to form a ring, sl st in back bar of first ch to form a ring, linking the Large Charm and Large Link together. Being careful not to twist the ch as you work, ch 1, working in back bar of sts, sc in each ch around. Invisible Fasten Off.

FASTENING DOME

With A, make a Magic Ring.

Rnd 1: Insert hook into ring, yo and draw up a lp, work 15 dc in the ring, join with a sl st in 2nd dc of rnd. Pull on tail end of yarn to close ring.

Rnd 2: Ch 1, sc in same st, then sc in each st around, join with a sl st in first sc.

Rnd 3: Sl st in every other st around to close up dome. Fasten off A.

FINISHING

Sew the Fastening Dome to the Large Link on the end that is opposite to the Fastening loop. Weave in ends. Sew a large pearl in the center of Large Charm, and a small pearl in the center of each of the Medium Charms. Pin out bracelet on a blocking board and wet or steam block.

Hairband Trio

Crochet cute, comfortable hairbands to accent and control her lovely locks. All three styles are worked with Pima Cotton, which has a soft sheen and holds its shape well. A classic bow is always a favorite to go with any outfit. Make just the bow to attach to any hairband, or cover a hairband completely with crochet, for a perfect match. An arrangement of cheerful daisies grace the side of this crochet covered band. A single daisy also makes a lovely hair clip! A sprinkle of dots across a crochet-covered hairband makes a classic accessory that is an ideal finishing touch. To make a band that will coordinate with many different outfits, crochet the dots in a variety of colors.

Special Stitches Used

- **Invisible Fasten Off (page 14)**
  Cut yarn leaving a 3" (7.5 cm) tail. Insert the hook into the blo of the first st in rnd, yo, and pull the yarn all the way through the loop on hook, as if to fasten off in the usual way. Insert hook in both lps of next st, yo with tail end and pull through st. Finally, insert the hook in the flo of last st in rnd, yo, pull yarn down through.

Skill Level
Easy

Gauge
20 hdc sts = 4" (10 cm) for the Band Cover. 13 sts = 2" (5 cm) for Bow Loops on the Bow Band. Take time to check gauge.

Yarn

Cascade Yarns Ultra Pima, 100% Pima Cotton, 220 yd (200 m)/3.5 oz (100 g)

Bow Band
1 skein #3704 Syrah

Daisy Band
1 skein each #3746 Chartreuse (A), #3718 Natural (B) and #3764 Sunshine (C)

Polka Dot Band
1 skein each #3764 Sunshine (A) and #3718 Natural (B)

Tools
C/2 (2.75 mm) crochet hook

D/3 (3.25 mm) crochet hook

yarn needle

rust-proof pins

hairband that measures 14⅜" (36.5 cm) from end to end, is ⅜" (1 cm) wide at the ends, and ¾" (2 cm) wide in the middle.

BOW BAND

Band Cover

With C/2 (2.75 mm) hook, ch 77.

Row 1: Working in back bar of ch sts, sc in 2nd ch from hook, sc in each of next 5 ch, hdc in next 16 ch, dc in foll 32 ch, hdc in next 16 ch, sc in last 6 ch, turn—76 sts.

Rows 2–5: Ch 1, sc in first 6 sts, hdc in next 64 sts, sc in last 6 sts, turn.

Row 6: Ch 1, sc in first 6 sts, hdc in next 16 sts, dc in next 32 sts, hdc in next 16 sts, sc in last 6 sts. Fasten off, leaving a 30" (76 cm) sewing length.

Bow Middle

Ch 110.

Row 1: Working in blo of ch sts, sl st in blo of 2nd ch from hook, sl st in blo of each ch across. Fasten off, leaving a 5" (13 cm) sewing length—109 sl sts.

Top Loops

Finished size: 3⅞" (10 cm)

Ch 48. Turn ch over to work in the back bars on the underside of the ch, being careful not to twist the ch, sl st in first ch to form a ring.

Rnd 1: Ch 1, working in back bar of ch sts, sc in same ch, sc in each ch around, join with a sl st in first sc—48 sc.

Rnds 2–4: Ch 1, sc in each st around, join with a sl st in first sc.

Rnd 5: Rep Rnd 2. Invisible Fasten Off.

Middle Loops

Finished size: 4¼" (11 cm)

Ch 54.

Rep Rnds 1–5 of Top Band—54 sc.

Bottom Loops

Finished size: 4¾" (12 cm)

Ch 60.

Rep Rnds 1–5 of Top Band—59 sc.

Finishing

Weave in all loose ends, except the tails of the Band Cover and Bow Middle. Block the Top, Middle, and Bottom Loops by spraying them with water, then, form them into a bow shape by pressing them down in the center and opening up the loops on each side.

Block the Bow Middle and Band Cover, by spraying them with water and pinning them out straight on a blocking board. Allow all of the pieces to dry completely before removing the pins. Wrap the Band Cover around the hairband and neatly sew the long edges together, centering the seam on the underside. Stack the Top, Middle, and Bottom Loops, and stitch them together in the center. Place the group of Loops on the side, 3¼" (8.5 cm) from one end of the band, and neatly and tightly wrap the Bow Middle cord around the stack and hairband five times. Sew the Bow Middle to the Loops, securing it to the hairband.

DAISY BAND

Band Cover

Make Band Cover following directions for Bow Band.

Small Daisy (Make 2)

With C/2 (2.75 mm) hook and B, make a Magic Ring (page 15).

Rnd 1: Insert hook in ring, yo and draw up a lp, ch 1, work 13 sc in ring, join with a sl st in first sc. Pull on tail end of yarn to close ring.

Rnd 2: *Ch 7, working in the back bar of the ch sts, sc in 2nd ch from hook, hdc in each ch across, sl st in same st in Rnd 1, sl st in next st, rep from * around. Fasten off.

Large Daisy

With C/2 (2.75 mm) hook and B, make a Magic Ring.

Rnd 1: Insert hook into ring, yo and draw up a lp, ch 1, work 18 sc in ring, join with a sl st in first sc.

Pull on tail end of yarn to close ring.

Rnd 2: *Ch 9, working in the back bar of the ch sts, sc in 2nd ch from hook, hdc in next ch, dc in each of next 5 ch, hdc in last ch, sl st in same st in Rnd 1, sl st in next st, rep from * around. Fasten off.

Small Daisy Center (Make 2)

With D/3 (3.25mm) hook and C, make a magic ring.

Rnd 1: Insert hook in ring, yo and draw up a lp, ch 1, work 6 sc in ring, join with a sl st in first sc. Pull on tail end of yarn to close ring.

Rnd 2: Ch 1, sc in first st, 2 sc in each sts around—11 sc.

Rnd 3: Ch 1, working in blo of sts, sc in each st around. Invisible Fasten Off.

Large Daisy Center

With D/3 (3.25mm) hook and C, make a magic ring.

Rnds 1–2: Rep Rnds 1–2 of Small Daisy Center.

Rnd 3: Ch 1, sc in first st, *sc in next st, 2 sc in next st, rep from * around, join with a sl st in first sc—16 sts.

Rnd 4: Ch 1, working in blo of sts, sc in each st around. Invisible Fasten Off.

Finishing

Using a yarn needle, weave in all ends except long tails of the Hairband Cover, and the tail ends of the Small and Large Daisies. Pin out all pieces on a blocking board and wet or steam block. Allow all of the pieces to dry completely before removing the pins. Attach Band Cover to hairband, following directions for Bow Band. Using invisible nylon thread and a sewing needle, sew the Small Daisy Centers to the middle of the Small Daisies, and the Large Daisy Center to the Large Daisy. Stitch the middle of one Small Daisy 7¼" (18.5 cm) from the right end of the hairband, then sew the middle of the Large Daisy 2½" (6.5 cm) down from the middle of Small Daisy. Sew the middle of the last Small Daisy 2½" (6.5 cm) down from the middle of the Large Daisy.

POLKA DOT BAND

Band Cover

Make Band Cover following directions for Bow Band.

Dots (Make 6)

With D/3 (3.25mm) hook and B, make a magic ring.

Rnd 1: Insert hook into ring, yo and draw up a lp, ch 1, work 8 sc in ring, join with a sl st in first sc. Pull on tail end of yarn to close ring.

Finishing

Pin out the Band Cover on a blocking board, and wet or steam block. Allow all of the pieces to dry completely before removing the pins. Attach Band cover to hairband following directions for Bow Band. Using a yarn needle, weave in ends on Dots. Using invisible nylon thread and a sewing needle, sew the Dots to the band, placing the first Dot on each side 3¾" (9.5 cm) from the ends of the band and the remaining four Dots equally spaced between.

Festival Hairband Stand

Practice a little upcycling by a crocheting a decorative covering for an oatmeal container, to make a regal hairband stand for the princess in your life. Give old hairbands a new look, by tightly wrapping them with one or more colors of yarn, until they are completely covered.

Special Stitches Used

- **Invisible Fasten Off (page 14)**
  Cut yarn leaving a 3" (7.5 cm) tail. Insert hook in blo of first st in rnd, yo, and draw yarn all the way through the loop on the hook, as if to fasten off in the usual way. Insert the hook in both lps of next st, yo with tail end and pull through st. Finally, insert hook in flo of last st in rnd, yo, draw yarn down through.

- **popcorn**
  Work 4 dc in designated st, drop lp from hook, insert hook in first dc, place dropped lp back on hook and draw through dc.

Skill Level
Easy

Finished Measurements
10½" (26.5 cm) long x 5½" (14 cm) high

Gauge
18 sts and 13 rows in hdc = 4" (10 cm)

Yarn

![4]

Berroco Weekend, 75% acrylic, 25% Peruvian cotton, 205 yd (188 m)/3.5 oz (100 g): 1 skein each #5956 Swimming Hole (A), #5926 Clothesline (B), and #5964 Curry (C)

Tools
D/3 (3.25 mm) crochet hook

E/4 (3.5 mm) crochet hook

pen

yarn needle

sewing needle

invisible nylon thread

rust-proof pins

empty oatmeal container 10" (25.5 cm) tall x 5¼" (13.5 cm) in diameter

½ yd (45.5 cm) light-weight quilt batting

cardboard

clear packing tape

BODY OF STAND

Lay out the quilt batting, and place the oatmeal container on top. Trace around the top of the container and the bottom of the container 2 times each. Cut out the 4 circles. Next, cut a piece of quilt batting that is 16½" (42 cm) x 9½" (23.5 cm), and another that is 16½" (42 cm) x 9⅛" (23 cm). Trace the bottom of the container onto a piece of cardboard and cut it out. Place the cardboard circle on the bottom of the container and secure it with tape. Next, wrap the smaller rectangle of quilt batting around the container, placing it just below the bottom edge of the plastic lid and pin the ends together. Use a sewing needle and invisible nylon thread to stitch the two ends together. Wrap the larger rectangle of quilt batting around the container on top of the first layer of quilt batting. Pin the ends together, and sew the ends together as before. Finally, sew 2 circles of batting to their respective ends of the container, covering the container completely with quilt batting.

With D/3 (3.25 mm) hook and A, ch 78.

Row 1: Working in back bars of ch sts, hdc in 3rd ch from hook, hdc in each each ch across, turn—76 hdc. **Note:** *Ch 2 at beginning of each row does not count as a st, here and throughout.*

Rows 2–33: Ch 2, hdc in each st across, turn. Do not turn at end of last row. Fasten off, leaving a 21" (53.5 cm) sewing length.

ENDS

With B, make a Magic Ring.

Rnd 1: With D/3 (3.25mm) hook, insert hook into ring, yo and pull up a lp, ch 2, work 9 hdc in ring, join with a sl st in first hdc. Pull on tail end of yarn to close ring—9 hdc.

Rnd 2: Ch 2, hdc in first st, then, 2 hdc in each st around, join with a sl st in first hdc—17 hdc.

Rnd 3: Ch 2, hdc in first st, *hdc in next, 2 hdc in foll, rep from * around, join with a sl st in first hdc—25 hdc.

Rnd 4: Ch 2, hdc in first st, *hdc in next 2 sts, 2 hdc in foll, rep from * around, join with a sl st in first hdc—33 hdc.

Rnd 5: Ch 2, hdc in first st, *hdc in next 3 sts, 2 hdc in foll, rep from * around. Sl st in beg hdc to close rnd—41 hdc.

Rnd 6: Ch 2, hdc in first st, *hdc in next 4 sts, 2 hdc in foll, rep from * around, join with a sl st in first hdc—49 hdc.

Rnd 7: Ch 2, hdc in first st, *hdc in next 5 sts, 2 hdc in foll, rep from * around, join with a sl st in first hdc—57 hdc. Fasten off B, join C in first st.

Rnd 8: With C, ch 3, 2 dc in first st, drop lp from hook, insert hook in third ch of beg ch-3, place dropped lp back on hook and draw through st (beg popcorn made), ch 2, sk next st, *popcorn in next st, ch 2, sk next st, rep from * around, change to B in the last st.

Rnd 9: With B, ch 2, *hdc in next popcorn, working over Rnd 8, hdc next skipped hdc from Rnd 7, rep from * around, join with a sl st in first hdc. Fasten off B, join A in first st.

Rnd 10: With A, ch 1, sc in same st, then sc in next 6 sts, 2 sc in next st, *sc in each of next 7 sts, 2 sc in next st, rep from * around, join with a sl st in first sc. Invisible Fasten Off—63 sts.

SCROLL BASE

With D/3 (3.25 mm) hook and C, ch 92.

Row 1: Working in the bar bars of ch sts, hdc in 3rd ch from hook, hdc in each ch across, turn.

Rows 2–3: Ch 2, hdc in each st across, turn. Do not turn at end of last row.

Row 4: Change to E/4 (3.50 mm) hook, *work 2 sc in corner st, working across side of strip, work 2 sc evenly spaced across, 2 sc in next corner*, working across opposite side of foundation ch on bottom edge, sl st in each ch across, rep from * to *once, working across top edge of piece, sl st in each st across. Invisible Fasten Off.

FLOWER (MAKE 2)

With A, make a Magic Ring (page 15).

Rnd 1: With D/3 (3.25 mm) hook, insert hook in ring, yo and pull up a lp, [ch 22, sl st in ring] 6 times. Pull on tail end of yarn to close ring. Fasten off A.

Flower Center (Make 2)

With C, make a Magic Ring.

Rnd 1: With D/3 (3.25 mm) hook, insert hook in ring, yo and pull up a lp, ch 2, work 7 hdc in ring, join with a sl st in first hdc. Pull on tail end of the yarn to close ring. Invisible Fasten Off.

FINISHING

Weave in ends. Next, pin out pieces on a blocking board, and wet or steam block. Then, sew the Flower Centers to the middle of the Flowers, with a sewing needle and invisible thread. Sew a flower to the center of each End piece. Pin the short ends of the Body of Stand together and sew the seam together. Slide this piece over the container to cover it. Sew the ends to the Body of Stand. Fold each of the Scroll Base pieces in half and place pins to mark the center, then measure 7" (18 cm) from each end of pieces and place pins as markers. With the WS of the Scroll Base pieces facing up, roll up each end to the pin marker. Remove the pin and replace it in the same spot, to secure the scroll in place. Sew through each scroll several times to secure. Finally, place the Scroll Base pieces on the underside of the stand, matching the center marker pins to the seam of the Body of Stand, placing them right up to the front edges of the stand. Sew Scroll Base pieces onto the front and back edges.

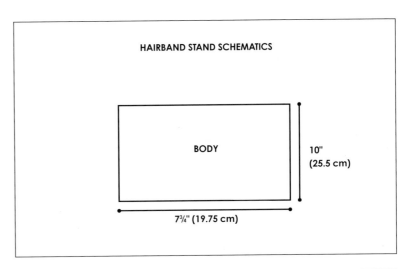

HAIRBAND STAND SCHEMATICS

BODY

10" (25.5 cm)

7¾" (19.75 cm)

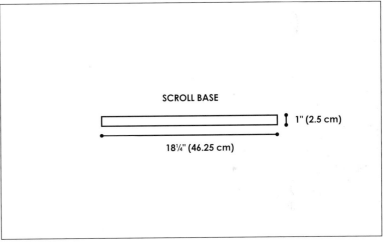

SCROLL BASE

1" (2.5 cm)

18¼" (46.25 cm)

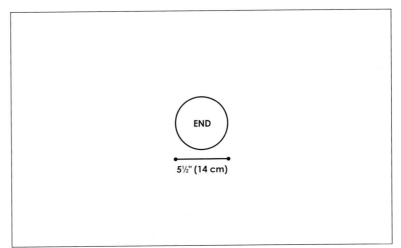

END

5½" (14 cm)

Buttons and Streamers Belt

Buttons and streamers are perfect partners, and together they make a jaunty child's belt. Simple stitches layered in an innovative way form the oversize buttons, and a little slip stitch fringe forms the festive tie. For a simplified version, make just the belt strip with streamers in her favorite colors.

Special Stitches Used

- *Invisible Fasten Off (page 14)*
  Cut the yarn, leaving a 3" (7.5 cm) tail. Insert the hook into the blo of the first st in rnd, yo, and pull the yarn all the way through the loop on the hook, as if to fasten off in the usual way. Insert the hook in both lps of next st, yo with tail end and pull through st. Finally, insert the hook in the flo of last st in rnd, yo, pull yarn down through.

Skill Level
Easy

Finished Sizes
Directions are given for child's size 6. Changes for 8 and 10 are in parentheses.

Finished Waist: 22½ (23½, 24½)" (57 [59.5, 62] cm)

Finished Measurements: Belt Strip with fringe measures 49½ (50½, 53)" (125.5 [128.5, 134.5] cm) long. Buttons = 2¼" (5.5 cm); Ring Links = 1⅛" (3 cm) in diameter.

Gauge
Buttons = 2¼" (5.5 cm) in diameter; Ring Links = 1⅛" (3 cm) in diameter; 31 sts = 4" (10 cm) in fringe pattern.

Yarn

Berroco Weekend DK, 75% acrylic, 25% Peruvian cotton, 268 yd (245 m)/3.5 oz (100 g): 1 skein each #2955 Reddy (A), #2972 Marigold (B), #2923 Tomatillo (C), and #2957 Grape (D)

Tools
C/2 (2.75 mm) crochet hook
D/3 (3.25 mm) crochet hook
yarn needle
rust-proof pins

BELT STRIP

With C/2 (2.75mm) hook and A, ch 110 (110, 115).

Row 1: Working in back bars of ch sts, sc in 2nd ch from hook and in each ch across, turn—109 (109, 114). Fasten off A, join B.

Row 2: With B, ch 1, sc in each sc across, turn. Fasten off B, join C.

Rows 3–5: Rep Row 2, working 1 row C, 1 rows D and 1 row A. Do not fasten off.

FRINGE

Continuing in yarn A, ch 106 (112, 118), working in blo of ch sts, sl st in 2nd ch from hook and in each ch across, sl st back in same st in Belt Strip. Fasten off—One fringe strand completed. Matching Fringe to row color, work a fringe strand at the end of each row of Belt Strip as follows: Join yarn with a sl st in the end of the row, ch 106 (112, 118), working in blo of ch sts, sl st in 2nd ch from hook and in each ch across, sl st back in same st in Belt Strip.

BUTTONS

Make 2 (2, 3) with A, 2 with B, 2 with D

With C/2 (2.75mm) hook, make a Magic Ring (page 15).

Rnd 1: Insert hook in ring, yo and pull up a lp, ch 2 (does not count as a st), work 9 hdc into ring, join with a sl st in first hdc. Pull on tail end of yarn to close ring.

Rnd 2: Ch 2, hdc in first st, 2 hdc in each st around, join with a sl st in first hdc—17 sts.

Rnd 3: Rep row 2—31 sts.

Rnd 4: Ch 2, hdc in each st around join with a sl st in first hdc. Invisible Fasten Off.

Rnd 5: Change to D/3 (3.25mm) hook. With RS facing, surface crochet in sts from Rnd 3 by inserting hook in a st from front to back, holding yarn under work, yo, draw up a lp. *insert hook in next st in Rnd 3, yo, draw up a lp, then draw lp through lp on hook, rep from * around. Pull the tail end of the yarn up to the top surface of your work, then work an Invisible Fasten Off.

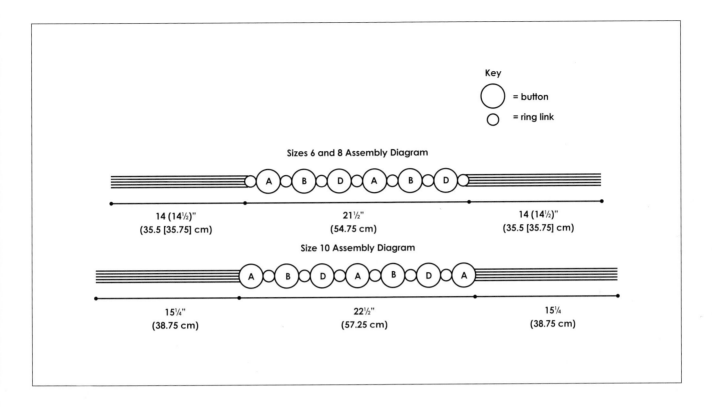

Key

= button

= ring link

Sizes 6 and 8 Assembly Diagram

| A | B | D | A | B | D |

14 (14½)"
(35.5 [35.75] cm)

21½"
(54.75 cm)

14 (14½)"
(35.5 [35.75] cm)

Size 10 Assembly Diagram

| A | B | D | A | B | D | A |

15¼"
(38.75 cm)

22½"
(57.25 cm)

15¼
(38.75 cm)

Rnd 6: Working in the sts formed in Rnd 5, yo twice around hook (instead of making a slip knot and a yo), work a standing dc in any st in Rnd 5, dc in each st around, join with a sl st in first dc.

Rnd 7: *Note:* *This rnd will join rnds 4 and 6 together.* *Insert hook in next st and in st that is directly across from it in Rnd 4, work a sl st, rep from * around. Cut the yarn, leaving a 3" (7.5) tail. Pull the tail end of the yarn up to the top surface of your work, then work and Invisible Fasten Off.

RING LINK

Make 7 (7, 6) with C.

With C/2 (2.75mm) hook, make a Magic Ring.

Rnd 1: Insert hook in ring, yo and draw up a lp, ch 1, work 21 sc in ring. Pull on tail end of yarn to tighten ring. Cutting yarn to a 12" (30 cm) in length, work an Invisible Fasten Off. Pull long yarn tail to backside of Ring Link. Working on the WS of the Ring Link, insert hook into st that is below the front lp of the last st worked in rnd, yo and draw

up a lp, ch 6, sk next 10 sts in ring, sl st in st that is just below the front lp of the next st. Sl st in the blo of each ch across. Fasten off.

FINISHING

With 2 strands of C, and a yarn needle, embroider an "X" in the center of each Button. Weave in ends. Using two strands of yarn in the Button color, sew the Buttons to the Ring Links following the assembly diagram for placement. Insert the Belt Strip into the vertical bars in the back of the Ring Links. Sew the first and last Ring Links (sizes 6 and 8)/ Buttons (size 10) to the ends of the belt, where the fringe begins. Pin belt out straight on a blocking board, and wet or steam block. Finally, tack each Button and Ring Link to the Belt Strip to secure.

Yarn Sources

Berroco Inc.
401-769-1212
1-800-343-4948
www.berroco.com

Cascade Yarns
206-574-0440
www.cascadeyarns.com

Classic Elite Yarns
1-800-343-0308
www.classiceliteyarns.com

Lion Brand Yarn Company
212-243-8995 x182
www.lionbrand.com

Universal Yarn
704-789-9276
877-864-9276
www.universalyarn.com

Spud & Chloë Yarns
www.spudandchloe.com

Red Heart
Coats & Clark
www.coatsandclark.com

Lily and Patons
www.sugarncream.com

Tahki Stacy Charles, Inc
www.tahkistacycharles.com

Rowan
www.knitrowan.com

About the Authors

Shelby Allaho holds a degree in fashion design, and has worked as an art department director for an embroidery design firm. She has won numerous design awards, and has exhibited her crochet work internationally. Her designs have been published in popular crochet magazines and books such as *Interweave Crochet*, *Inside Crochet*, and *Runway Crochet* by Margaret Hubert, published by CPi. She enjoys promoting the art of crochet through social media and on her blog, www.stitch-story.com.

One of my biggest crochet career goals was to write a book, and I am thrilled that this dream has been realized. First of all, I would like to thank my beloved grandmothers, Evelyn Biehn and Joan McCornack. Evelyn taught me to crochet and to love the craft, and Joan was a true creative inspiration who taught me so much about the textile arts. I would also like to thank my dear parents, Stewart and Carol McCornack, for their years of support and for helping me pursue my dream of studying fashion design; my motivational aunt, Julie Anne Sadie, for all of her encouragement in my creative endeavors; my wonderful mentor, Margaret Hubert, for believing in me and introducing me to our marvelous editor, Linda Neubauer; and last but never least, my loving husband and best friend Emad and my precious daughter Sara, for their amazing support and understanding. I feel very fortunate that I'm able to do what I love, and to have people in my life who have helped make this possible. —Shelby

Ellen Gormley stitched more than 80 afghans before beginning her design career in 2004. Now, Ellen has sold more than 200 designs and been published numerous times in many crochet magazines including *Interweave Crochet*, *Crochet Today*, *Crochet!*, *Crochet World*, and *Inside Crochet*. Ellen is a crochet expert on *Knit & Crochet Now*. She is the online teacher of *Annie's Crocheting with Beads*. Her two books are *Go Crochet! Afghan Design Workbook* and *Learn Bruges Lace*. She was also a contributing designer for Margaret Hubert's *Runway Crochet*. You can follow Ellen on her blog at www.GoCrochet.com and as "GoCrochet" on Twitter and www.Ravelry.com.

Thank you to God who has given me the inspiration and skills to do what I love. Thank you to my husband, Tom, who works hard to provide for us so I can have it all. Thank you to our kids, Maura and Patrick, who cook dinner when I'm pushing a deadline and wind my yarn when I'm in a hurry. You both are smart, talented kids and your potential is unlimited! —Ellen

Index